Helion & Company Limited
Unit 8 Amherst Business Centre
Budbrooke Road
Warwick
CV34 5WE
England
Tel. 01926 499 619
Email: info@helion.co.uk
Website: www.helion.co.uk
Twitter: @helionbooks
Visit our blog http://blog.helion.co.uk/

Original edition co-published by Helion & Company Limited and 30° South Publishers (Pty) Limited 2011. This revised edition published by Helion & Company Limited 2019

This edition incorporates elements designed and typeset by 30° South Publishers (Pty) Limited. Additional typesetting by Farr out Publications, Wokingham, Berkshire
Cover designed by Paul Hewitt, Battlefield Design (www.battlefield-design.co.uk)
Printed by Henry Ling Limited, Dorchester, Dorset

ISBN 978-1-915070-57-9

British Library Cataloguing-in-Publication Data.
A catalogue record for this book is available from the British Library.

CONTENTS

Note: In order to simplify the use of this book, all names, locations and geographic designations are as provided in *The Times World Atlas*, or other traditionally accepted major sources of reference, as of the time of described events. Correspondingly, the term 'Congo' designates the area of the former Belgian colony of the Congo Free State, granted independence as the Democratic Republic of the Congo in June 1960 and in use until 1971 when the country was renamed Republic of Zaire, which, in turn, reverted to Democratic Republic of the Congo in 1997, and which remains in use today. As such, Congo is not to be mistaken for the former French colony of Middle Congo (Moyen Congo), officially named the Republic of the Congo on its independence in August 1960, also known as Congo-Brazzaville.

GLOSSARY

AC-130 – Lockheed gunship
ARFOR – Army Force Somalia
AWWSS – Authorized Weapons Storage Site
'Black Sea' – A central market district in the heart of Aidid's (SNA) sector of Somalia
C-130 – Hercules transport aircraft
CENTCOM – US Central Command
CIA – Central Intelligence Agency
CINCCENT – Commander in Chief, US Central Command
COMUSFORSOM – Command US Forces Somalia
CSAR – combat search and rescue
HRO – Humanitarian Relief Organization
HUMINT – Human Intelligence
ISE – Intelligence Support Element
JOC – Joint Operations Centre
JSOC – Joint Special Operations Command
JSOT – Joint Special Operations Tactics
JSOTF – Joint Special Operations Task Force
JTF – Joint Task Force Somalia
K4 – Kilometer 4, a key traffic circle in Mogadishu and a junction of several major roads
khat – a narcotic plant widely used in Somalia
'Mad Mullah' – the name given to early Somali resistance leader Mohammed Abdullah Hassan
MARFOR – Marine Force Somalia
MEF – Marine Expeditionary Force
MEU – Marine Expeditionary Unit
NCO – non-commissioned officer
NGO – non-governmental organization
OAU – Organization of African Unity
OPCON – operational control
POTF – Psychological Operations Task Force
QRF – quick reaction force
Redcon 1 – full alert level
RPG – rocket-propelled grenade
Schutztruppe – German native colonial unit
SEAL – Sea/Air/Land US Naval Special Forces
'skinny' – pejorative military term for Somali militiaman
SNA – Somali National Alliance
SNF – Somali National Front
SNM – Somali National Movement
SPM - Somali Patriotic Movement
SSDF – Somali Salvation Democratic Front
SSF – Somali Salvation Front
TACON – tactical control
Triangle of Death – the most famine-affected region of Somalia, between Mogadishu, Baidoa and Bardera
UN – United Nations
UNITAF – United Task Force
UNOSOM – United Nations Operation in Somalia
USAF – United States Air Force
USC – United Somali Congress
USFORSOM – US Forces Somalia
USSOCOM – United States Special Operations Command

German soldiers onboard an armoured personnel carrier (APC) on hand for the dedication of a well, which they dug for the Somalis. Germany's defence minister dedicated the well as part of his nation's contribution to the relief effort.

INTRODUCTION

Me and my clan against the world, me and my brother against the clan, me against my brother
– Somali proverb

In 1855, British soldier, explorer, author and essayist, Richard Francis Burton, attempted the first organized exploration of Somalia. He travelled in the company of a handful of fellow British army officers, including his long-time companion and part-time antagonist, John Speke, with whom he would later break over that great geographic conundrum of the time, the source of the Nile. The journey had no sooner begun, than the large travelling party was attacked by some 300 natives who overran the camp in the dead of night, creating general mayhem and severely injuring both Burton and Speke. Speke was wounded eleven times, and Burton himself suffered the very unpleasant experience of a spear through both cheeks, knocking out four teeth and piercing his palate. Thanks to a barb on the blade, Burton was unable to remove the head of the spear, which he then endured embedded in his face for several days until he was able to make his way to the British Red Sea port of Aden.

It is fair to assume that this experience would have jaded him somewhat in his opinions of the Somalis, but even with this in mind, and despite several Kiplingesque attempts to forgive the noble savage his savagery, his later published account, *First Footsteps in East Africa*, is rich with observations of the general violence, duplicity and debilitating self-interest that appeared to characterize the Somali clansman at the time.

> In character, the Isa [a Somali clan] are childish and docile, cunning, and deficient in judgment, kind and fickle, good-humoured and irascible, warm-hearted, and infamous for cruelty and treachery.[1]

Above: Richard Francis Burton

Left: John Hanning Speke

This outside view of Somalia has been similarly expressed in countless chronicles ever since, even those written under the rules of absolute political correctness. For example, US academic Jonathan Stevenson, one of a great many writers who

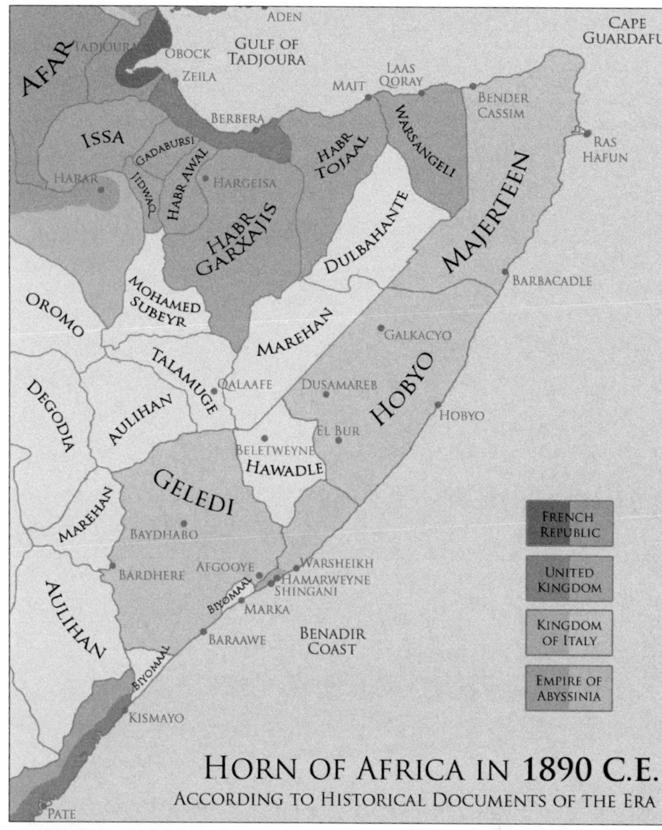

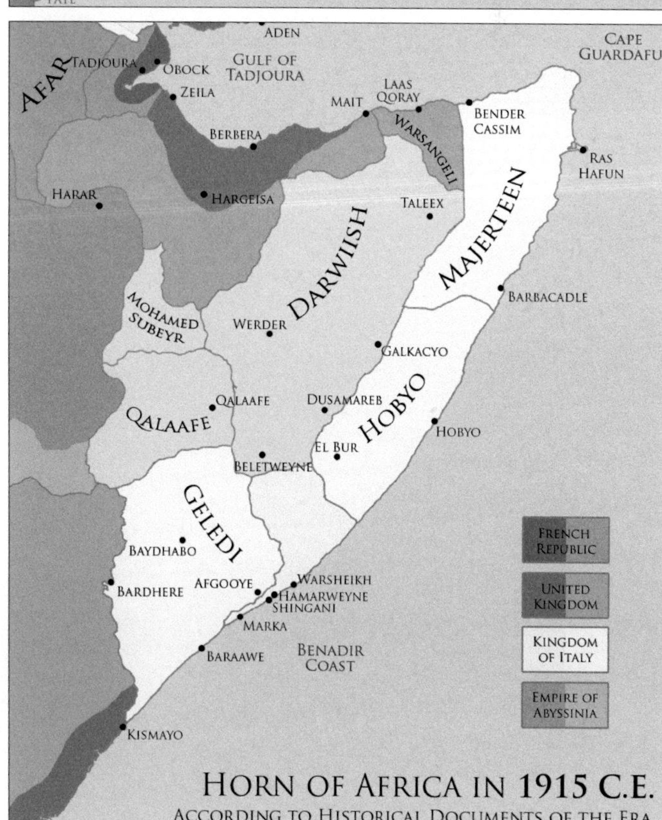

have covered Somalia in recent years, opens an extremely well-observed narrative, *Losing Mogadishu*, with the remark that it is Somali culture that makes Somalis so singularly unmalleable, so reluctant to take guidance. He then goes on to freely paint a very bleak picture of a callous, individualistic, violent and intensely xenophobic society, caught at the genealogical crossroads of two dominant societies – they regard Arabs as gifted brothers and black Africans as handicapped cousins – and with inferiority as just one of a plethora of debilitating social complexes.[2]

However, even for a lay student of world affairs, observations such as these seem to have an authentic ring. News emerging from the country on a daily basis does tend to leave very little room for any improved perception, for, although the surface impressions of universal lawlessness, hyper-violence and social chaos might be unjust, Somalia is still a deeply troubled society.

Somalia crept into the general global consciousness during the early 1990s, as news images of yet another distant and incomprehensible bout of African warfare gradually began to

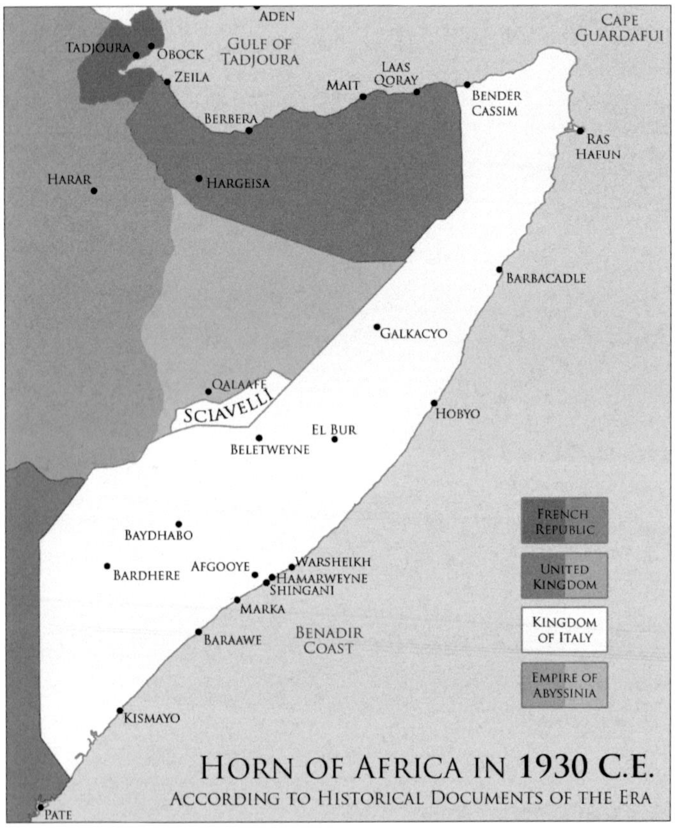

Horn of Africa in 1930 C.E.
According to Historical Documents of the Era

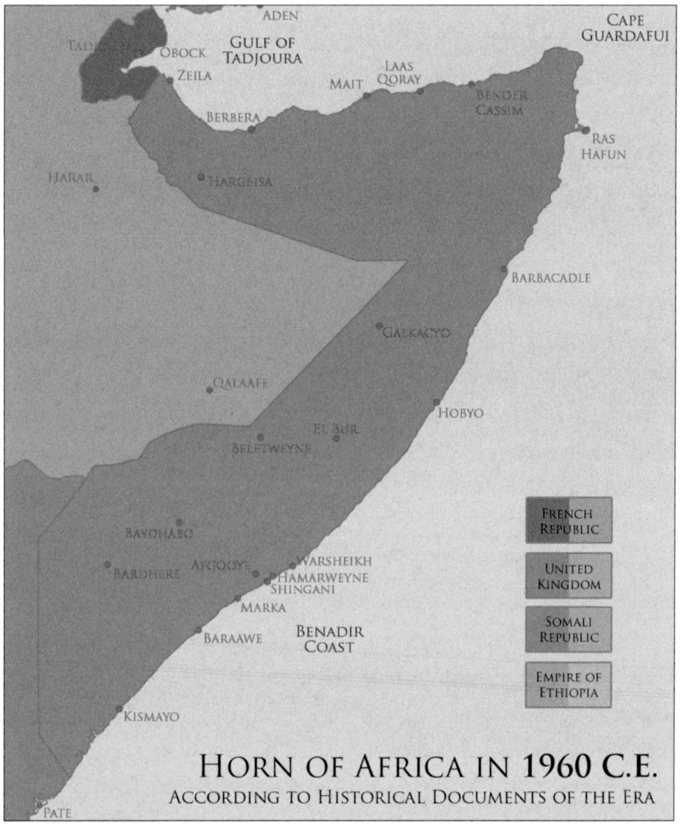

Horn of Africa in 1960 C.E.
According to Historical Documents of the Era

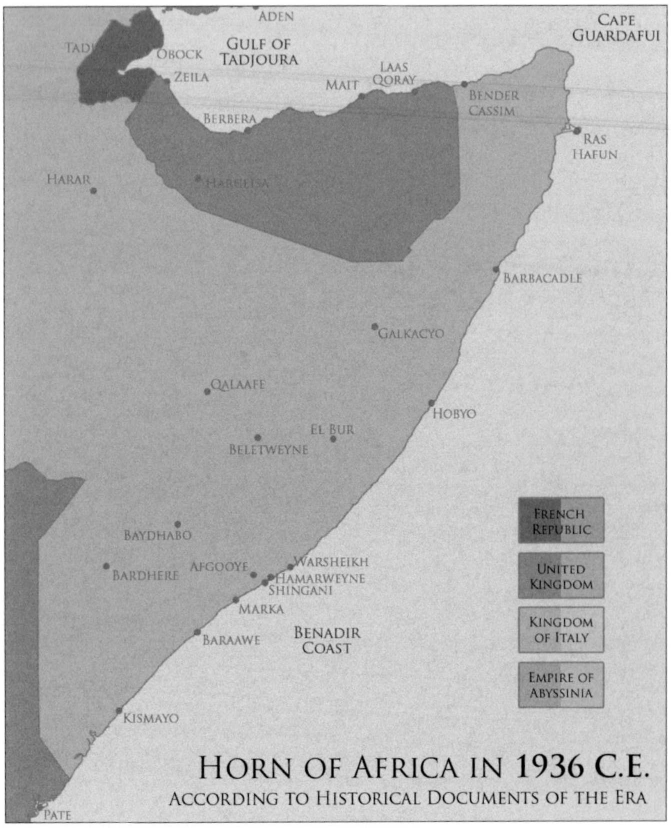

Horn of Africa in 1936 C.E.
According to Historical Documents of the Era

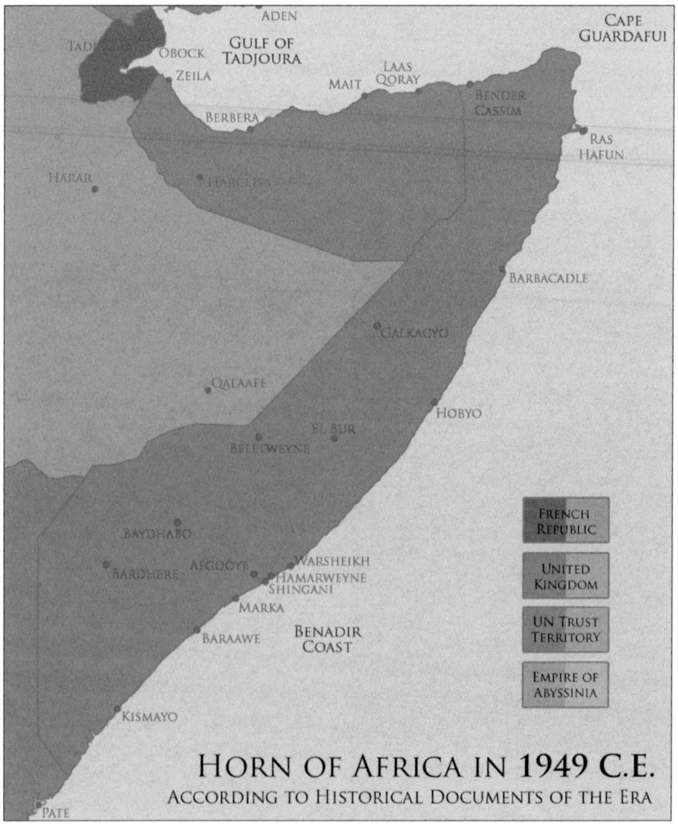

Horn of Africa in 1949 C.E.
According to Historical Documents of the Era

assume the proportions of mass dislocation, complete social breakdown and epidemic hunger. Even this, however, bearing in mind the experience of Ethiopia just a decade earlier, might easily have been blurred within the general clamour of news had it not been for the unexpected intrusion in October 1993 of images depicting US soldiers gunned down in the streets of Mogadishu, their bodies mutilated and dragged through the dust for a crime no greater than attempting to protect a nation against itself, and to feed the hungry masses.

It was at this point that a specific picture of Somalia, and Somalis in general, began to emerge in the western consciousness. The dark-skinned, angular-featured and gun-toting *skinny*, cruising ruined cities in armed *technicals* like extras in an apocalyptic movie, became an icon of the lawless Horn of Africa. Somalia emerged as a clear example of the potential risks of a marriage between anarchy and technology, leavened by astronomical self-interest and the unrestricted flow of illicit armaments from a collapsed Soviet Union. This image had about it a flavour of the human end-game, the practical results of an imploded society, not unlike the images emerging from Liberia, and later, Sierra Leone, of speed-fuelled and heavily armed gangs of prepubescent boys ranging the countryside like a living parody of *Lord of the Flies*. Moreover, there seemed to be a chillingly natural aura about it all, the obvious conclusion to a trajectory of self-destruction and anarchy that Africa – appearing as it did to the west as a homogenous mass – had for all intents and purposes been pursuing since the dawn of the liberation period. Somalia certainly was, and certainly had been a region of peculiar individuality that had defied efforts at central control, and at aligning the singularly perverse polarity of a multitude of individual clans. Europeans did not find the process of colonization easy and, in fact, Somalia was the only region on the continent to mount any kind of meaningful armed resistance to European occupation.

In general, the European expansion into Africa had been trouble-free. The ground rules and general boundary delineations had been predetermined during a summit of leading European heads of state held in Berlin during 1884/85, with the main proviso being proof of annexation before general recognition, and with annexation either being requested by native authority or deemed unilaterally to be in their interests. The process was, therefore, expedited by an army of treaty-gatherers who toured the remote regions of the continent, securing agreement for European protection, quite often under spurious terms, the conditions of which were usually exploited by a company of investors operating under the authority of a Royal Charter.

The principal nations involved in this process were Britain, France, Germany, Belgium and Portugal. Italy played a limited initial role in sub-Saharan Africa, but displayed a keen interest in the Horn, jostling within a tenuous memorandum of understanding with Britain over control and occupation of the region, later taking advantage of the shifting power dynamics that accompanied the rise of fascism in Europe to seize much of the landmass of Somalia and Ethiopia as a strategic springboard to

Statue of Sayyid Mohammed Abdullah Hassan (the 'Mad Mullah') in Mogadishu.

much grander scheme to forcibly assume the key assets of Britain in the region.

The territory of Greater Somalia, what would now consist of the entire area of modern-day Somalia, the Somali Republic, all of the Ethiopian region of Ogaden and a significant swathe of northeastern Kenya, fell under the administrative mandate of Britain, Italy and Ethiopia, the latter being recognized as a functioning dynastic monarchy in the European pattern, and not, at that point, subject to the threat of absolute colonial occupation itself.

The first attempts to practically pacify the territory were undertaken by the Ethiopians under Emperor Menelik II, which were unsuccessful, but which were followed by a 20-year combined campaign of attrition by British, Italian and Ethiopian forces, succeeding in pacifying the territory only in 1920, by use of an air bombardment of the Dervish capital of Taleex. This campaign was officially known as the Somaliland Campaign, but unofficially the Mad Mullah Campaign, thanks to the leadership of a powerful and messianic Somali religious leader, correctly known as Mohammed Abdullah Hassan. This campaign was sustained over five separate offensives, the last being that of 1920.*

Key to this final successful push into the Dervish heartland was a combination of Royal Air Force hardware and the traditional fighting platform of the Somaliland Camel Corps, one of the most interesting and heavily romanticized of a great many British colonial corps and regiments. It was an established practice during the colonial period to make use of indigenous local militias under European command to both secure and police subject territories. The Indian Army was an excellent example of this, but in the African context two extremely influential forces existed for a

* Mohammed Abdullah Hassan founded what became known as the Dervish State, a Somali Sunni Islamic state enforced by Somali fighting men drawn from across the Horn of Africa and known as the Dervishes. This large armed force enabled Mohammed Abdullah Hassan to establish a large subject territory.

considerable period, the first being the King's African Rifles, several battalions of which were distributed over a number of British territories, and the German *Schutztruppe*, a similarly configured native force that formed the backbone of the German defence of her African territories. This was particularly so during the First World War and most notably during the East Africa Campaign that was fought largely in the Tanganyika territory between the massed ranks of British and Commonwealth forces and a significant German native force, the Schutztruppe, which ceased to exist after 1918 and the defeat of Germany in Europe.

The Somaliland Camel Corps came into being upon the British annexation of British Somaliland, a swathe of territory corresponding with the current Somaliland Republic, and adjacent across the Gulf of Aden to the Indian-administered sea port of the same name. In 1898, administration of British Somaliland passed from the Indian government to the Foreign Office. Prior to this, the territory had, like Aden, been administered from India through an Indian political official known as the political resident for the Somali coast, assisted by local residents located in Zaila, Bulhar and Berbera. When administration of the territory was taken over by the Foreign Office, a consul-general with his residency in Berbera was appointed, and assisted by three similarly distributed vice-consuls.

The Camel Corps, in fact, began as a constabulary in order to utilize the natural affinity of the local herdsman with their camels, to introduce some law into an otherwise vast and lawless hinterland. The unit essentially comprised indigenous mounted infantrymen, along with British or colonial officers and senior NCOs. Prior to, and during the First World War, the constabulary applied itself primarily to the ongoing Mad Mullah affair, suffering a catastrophic defeat at the hands of the Dervishes in August 1913 that resulted in the deaths of 36 members out of a force of 110, including unit commander, Colonel Richard Corfield.

The main actions of the First World War in Africa were the South West Africa and East Africa campaigns that effectively removed Germany as a player in the great colonial game. It was not until after the war, during 1920 in fact, that the British administration was able to assemble sufficient force to finally defeat and destroy the Dervish State. The main force complement was the Royal Air Force, flying 12 new Airco DH.9A single-engined light bombers, ostensibly supporting ground forces, which comprised the Somaliland Camel Corps, a vehicle fleet and elements of the King's African Rifles.

The campaign that followed was spearheaded by highly successful air bombardments of enemy strongpoints, with follow-up ground actions that established the basics of later close-air-support tactics that would endure to this day. In a reasonably short order, the Mad Mullah was defeated and driven out of the territory, allowing for the establishment of a coherent civil administration and paving the way for the far greater mobilization of imperial force in the region that would take place during the Second World War.

The Italians, in general, had not fared well in the race for colonial territory in Africa, and had certainly achieved little in the Horn of Africa beyond the practical administration of the coast of southern Somalia, or Italian Somaliland. However, much more than this did Italy covet. The point of greatest strategic interest in the region was the peninsular itself, which lay under British control. The port of Berbera looked across the Mandab Strait to Aden on the Arabian mainland, also a British asset, supported

Airco DH.9A

A ship travelling through the Suez Canal, 1917.

Pavilion of the Suez Canal Company, Paris Exposition, 1889.

C Company 7th Battalion King's African Rifles (KAR) at Mogadishu, 1941.

Graves of Royal Natal Carabineers (South Africa), ambushed at Gelib, Somalia, 1941.

by France, Britain's partner in the *Compagnie de Suez*, from the enclave of Djibouti. The strategic value of this configuration, which allowed Britain and France to influence the health of global shipping, began to take on a far greater significance as Europe, and all the key players in Africa, began to arm for war.

Key to free access to the Suez Canal lay in control of the Mandab, but key to control of this vital waterway lay in control of Egypt, then also under British rule. Egypt was buffered by British Palestine to the east and French North Africa to the west, with the only potentially belligerent piece on the board being Italy, established as a colonial power in Libya. Then, in October 1935, the Italians finally moved aggressively against Ethiopia. With the highly controversial use of poison gas, the monarchy was overthrown and, in March of the following year, Italy officially occupied the territory.

With this, the African chessboard abruptly began to look very different. Brimming with élan, Mussolini then began to ponder Egyptian-administered Sudan, a sparsely garrisoned British territory now sandwiched between two Italian strongpoints, Libya and Ethiopia. Clearly, a strategy of linking up Libya and Ethiopia and gaining control of the Red Sea would throttle British Egypt, by then already beginning to suffer the effects of hostile shipping conditions in the Mediterranean. The practical potential of this goal was considerably enhanced with the outbreak of war and the quick collapse of France. Britain now stood alone in North Africa. With British troops crowding the beaches of Dunkirk, and overtures to the Battle of Britain already yielding to aerial pressure in the skies over Britain, and, moreover, with all possible resources diverted to Egypt, British Africa suddenly lay very vulnerable and dangerously exposed to the ballooning ambitions of a highly confident Benito Mussolini.

No small part of Mussolini's vision was the seizure of the unguarded fatted calf of British Africa. With colonial manpower flooding north to bolster the khaki line, nothing but a handful of insubstantial settler militias and native battalions lay between the southern boundary of Somaliland and the Limpopo River, most of which was British, with the rest being either French or Belgian. Thus, the immediate focus of war in Africa lay in East Africa and, in particular, in the sprawling twin territories of British and Italian Somaliland.

Concurrent with the mass mobilization and gargantuan battle scenarios beginning to unfold in North Africa, during which Italy would lose Libya, the stage was set for a much smaller, but no less concentrated, struggle in the Horn of Africa. Prior to this, a great deal of infrastructural development had taken place in Italian Somaliland. Most impressive was the outstanding military road system that was constructed both quickly and well from Massawa in Eritrea, through Addis Ababa, and southward to the Somali capital of Mogadishu. Military airfields, supported by a modern and comprehensive system of communication towers, were also strategically located to provide effective bomber access to points as far south as Mombasa, and as far west as Khartoum. By June 1940, Italian force of arms in East Africa comprised four command sectors, with a total of 300,000 men, falling under the direction of Prince Amadeo, the Duke of Aosta, and a cousin to the King of Italy.

In the order of things, however, before the Italians could mount an offensive against the soft underbelly of British Africa, the rather harder nut of seizing and securing British Somaliland had to be cracked. This presented something of a strategic conundrum for the British. British Somaliland fell under Middle East Command,

Air Chief Marshal Sir Robert Brooke-Popham, commander-in-chief Far East, and General Sir Archibald Wavell.

Talleh, British Somaliland. (National Archives, UK)

Lookout post in British Somaliland. (National Archives, UK)

headquartered in Cairo and commanded by General Sir Archibald Wavell. Wavell, at that time, had his hands full with operations both in North Africa and the Levantine, which left him with little resource to consider the defence of British Somaliland. To complicate this, British prime minister, Winston Churchill, was very much of the opinion that the loss of British overseas territory in war would set a morbid precedent for the defenders of the mainland, fighting and dying in the skies over England. In the event, the decision was taken to mount a limited defence, upon the understanding that the territory would be lost, but with the Italians being forced to pay heavily for every inch of territory.

The result was the celebrated Battle of Tug Argan, something of an enthusiast's favourite, which raged across central Somaliland between Hargeisa and Berbera, between 3 and 19 August 1940, concluding in the orderly embarkation and departure of all British forces for Aden, and the temporary re-badging of the territory Italian Somaliland.

The following month, September 1940, Italy launched an invasion of Egypt from Libya that began with much fanfare and expectation, but which was halted shortly afterwards, and then driven back by British forces who then occupied the territory. This effectively destroyed the individual territorial ambitions of the Italians, which were then subverted toward German interests, while the large Italian force located in Somalia and Ethiopia was immediately put on the defensive. A massive build-up of Allied force began in Kenya, comprising mostly native battalions under colonial command, but supported by a significant air, armour and infantry infusion from South Africa and various rear echelon RAF formations fielding older aircraft and dominated by Southern Rhodesian and South African pilots.

Much of the fight had been knocked out of the Italians by this time, and the Allied offensive, when it began in December 1940, very quickly devolved into a rout. Mechanized infantry and armour reached Kismayo in mid-February 1941, reaching and occupying Mogadishu soon afterwards. Then, with more realistic lines of supply, the campaign shifted northward, plunging forward up the superb *Strada Imperiale*, linking up with an Allied force moving in from the east, having retaken British Somaliland almost without a fight, reaching Addis Ababa on 26 March 1941.

Thereafter, the Italians were effectively out of Africa, and while the titanic struggle for control of Egypt continued, and as German fortunes waned, control of greater Somalia fell entirely into British hands. Many Italian colonists remained, however, and a UN trusteeship over the colony was eventually granted to Italy, although Britain remained the senior partner until independence and unification of British and Italian Somalia in 1960.

Indigenous government over a united Somalia was almost within itself an oxymoron. Traditionally, no central government or unified control had ever taken root in Somalia. The nomadic lifestyle and individualistic mindset characteristic of ethnic Somali clansmen, tended to preclude it. Historic attrition over water, livestock and other resources further complicated a bewildering ebb and flow of loyalties, enmities, alliances and conflicts, all of which spilled into post-independence politics, with the inevitable result that the ideal of national unity was quickly subverted to

Silsilad, British Somaliland. (National Archives, UK)

narrow clan interests. A plethora of competing political parties and the narrow distribution of patronage based on clan and family loyalties became the pattern leading up to a bloodless coup in October 1969 that transferred power from civilian to military leadership. The new government, scientific socialist in its stated ideological alignment, was headed by army commander, Major-General Mohamed Siad Barre.*

It is at this point that the fortunes of Somalia, now the Somali Democratic Republic, began to tilt towards anarchy. Initially, the signs were good. Siad Barre emphasized clan unity and development within a socialist framework that initially won him broad public support. With perhaps an exaggerated expectation of Soviet military support Siad Barre made a risky play on Somali patriotism by adopting an irredentist posture over the Ogaden, a large swath of territory nominally within Ethiopia, but populated by an ethnic Somali majority. The territory had been given to Ethiopia by the British in the aftermath of the Second World War, while repeated claims for its return by Somalia had been ignored. In what was initially a highly popular move, Siad Barre launched a 1977 war against Ethiopia to reclaim the territory for Somalia, a strategy which badly backfired when Soviet support in the region abruptly shifted from Somalia to Ethiopia in the aftermath of a successful overthrow of the monarchy, and its replacement by a communist-aligned military junta headed by Mengistu Haile Mariam. In response, Siad Barre evicted the Soviets from Somalia which precipitated a severe military rout.

All this took place as the global power dynamic, in general, was undergoing an abrupt realignment, with the Soviet invasion of Afghanistan, the overthrow of the Shah of Iran and the subsequent threat that both these events posed to the flow of oil from the Middle East. This placed Somalia at the crossroads of a new strategic configuration, which offered the opportunity for Siad Barre to court the United States, previously supportive of Haile Selassie against Soviet-supported Somalia, in a grand policy reversal that revealed an admirable flexibility of mind on the part of both the Carter administration and the embattled military regime in Mogadishu. The net result was the Carter Doctrine, a position declared by president of the United States Jimmy Carter in his State of the Union Address on 23 January 1980, in which he asserted the willingness of the United States to use military force, if necessary, to defend its national interests in the Persian Gulf region. This led to the creation of the Rapid Deployment Force, soon afterward renamed Central Command, or CENTCOM, followed by the establishment of a series of US military bases located in Diego Garcia in the mid-Indian Ocean, on the Island of Masirah off the coast of Oman and assuming the old Soviet port and air facilities located in Berbera, Somalia.[3] For the military regime in Somalia, and Siad Barre in particular, this offered a brief season under the sunshine of US military and development support. This kept the administration solvent and bolstered the ability of the military to respond both to low-level insurgencies mounted against the government from within Ethiopia, and to support armed Somali dissidents infiltrating the Ogaden to mount attacks against the Ethiopian military.

In the face of growing disaffection with the regime, and not withstanding its early disavowal of clan politics, Siad Barre began, increasingly, to rely on the manipulation of the clan system for its political survival. The Somali clan system was reflective of the ethnic and language diversity of Africa as a whole, a state of affairs that exposed most of the liberated nations of the continent to some degree of tribal or ethnic tension within government. Nineteenth-century European boundary demarcations had paid scant regard to the distribution of peoples and languages, with the result that often mutually antagonistic groups were locked together in a single nation, forming a recipe for ongoing tension in many places, and occasional bouts of equalization that resulted, usually, in a coup or a rebellion.

In Somalia, the dynamic was similar, but more concentrated. While most African populations would consider their tribal identity before they would their national identity, in Somalia the clan identity of a majority of the population was supreme, rendered even more sharply defined by the tendencies of the Siad Barre regime to politicize the clan structure, increasing tensions within the system and, moreover, lending almost absolute certainty to the fact that, when the whole broke apart, efforts to regain any

* The coup was not entirely bloodless. It was precipitated by the assassination of President Abdirashid Ali Sharmarke by one of his own bodyguards.

Military portrait of Major-General Mohamed Siad Barre

Mengistu Haile Mariam

Jimmy Carter, president of the United States

General Mohammed Farah Aidid

practical cohesion would be almost impossible. And this was indeed what proved to be the case. The Somali clan structure is configured along the broad lines of five principal clan families: the Hawiye, Darod, Isaaq, Dir and Rahanwein, all of which, according to tradition, share a common ancestor. Each clan is further divided into five or more smaller clans, which in turn are divided into numerous sub-clans. Siad Barre himself was a member of the Marehan, a sub-clan of the Darod.

Multiple clan-based insurgencies began almost as soon as the débâcle of the Ogaden War was over. A number of fairly narrowly defined political/insurgent fronts quickly emerged, beginning with the Somali Salvation Front (SSF), comprising mainly Majerteen military dissidents, which merged in October 1981 with a smaller splinter group to form the Somali Salvation Democratic Front (SSDF). Soon afterward, the Somali National Movement (SNM) was formed in London as a narrowly focused Isaaq movement, primarily representing the interests of the clansmen of the north. Both organizations operated from within Ethiopia, receiving political, financial and a limited amount of military support from Ethiopia and Libya, the latter by then deeply involved in a number of destructive civil wars and insurgencies across sub-Saharan Africa.

The SNM tended to be more successful, thanks to the material support of prosperous Isaaq communities scattered across the Gulf region, but neither really impacted the regime other than to invite more brutal and violent repression, in particular against the Isaaq in the north. The civil war proper began in May 1988 with the launch of a large-scale SNM offensive from within Ethiopia that attracted a disproportionately violent response from the government. Arial bombardments and civilian massacres drove some 300,000 Isaaqs to seek refuge in Ethiopia, while many thousands of others were displaced internally.

Over the course of the next few years, clan disaffection and clan-based insurgencies grew more widespread until, in 1992, a broad-based alliance of opposition forces was formed under the banner of the Somali National Alliance (SNA). Several key figures emerged from this process, perhaps most notable of whom was General Mohammed Farah Aidid (also Aideed), who would play a central role in the dramatic events of the next few years.

Aidid was in many ways an enigma, and in others simply a stereotypical Somali displaying actions, motivations and responses that were often incomprehensible to those attempting to deal with him on a military and diplomatic level. Born a Hawiye of the Habr Gidir clan, Aidid was possessed of certain key attributes common to the emerging political elite of Africa. He had been educated under the Italian system in Rome and Moscow, rose through the ranks of the local colonial police as, incidentally, had Siad Barre himself, graduating to the military where he served under temporary loyalty to Siad Barre, commanding troops during the Ogaden War. He later entered Siad Barre's political inner circle, serving both in the cabinet and as ambassador to India, before submerging into the murky depths of state intelligence as head of the National Security Service. From this position, Aidid very quickly began to represent a threat, and was dealt with by the customary accusations of plotting a coup – which he conceivably was – thanks to which he served a total of six years in prison.

By the advent of the 1990s, popular discontent had spread throughout the country, to the extent that Siad Barre found himself facing a general revolt. At the head of opposing USC forces was General Aidid, now Siad Barre's sworn enemy, who pressed in eastward towards Mogadishu from the Ethiopian border, capturing quantities of arms and equipment as he advanced, entering Mogadishu late in December 1990. The ministry of defence and the presidency were soon captured, yielding the insurgents much heavy weaponry. On 5 January 1991, US embassy staff and hundreds of foreign diplomats and relief workers were airlifted offshore to waiting US Navy ships. This left diplomatic compounds to be comprehensively looted to a degree that astonished journalists and diplomats in the months that followed.

In the meanwhile, on 27 January, Siad Barre fled the capital, taking with him everything that he could and travelling with a small loyal force. For a year or more, he and Aidid grappled across the arid expanses of south/central Somalia. Siad Barre attempted, unsuccessfully, to rally his forces and retake Mogadishu a month after his ouster and, thereafter, several bitter offensives played out, as the embattled ex-president fought to regain the advantage. As he did, he pursued a scorched earth policy across the region,

Javier Pérez de Cuéllar

Boutros Boutros-Ghali

Nicolae Ceausescu meets with Mohamed Siad Barre in Moscow on 4 March 1976. (Romanian Communism Online Photo Collection)

destroying boreholes and canals, which in turn completely disrupted the normal routines of agriculture, precipitating in large measure the desperate famine that would follow.

Heavy fighting took place around Kismayo and Baidoa, creating acute food insecurity in what later came to be known as the Triangle of Death in southern Somalia, demarcated generally by the settlements of Kismayo, Baidoa and Mogadishu. In May 1992, Siad Barre's depleted forces mounted a last substantive offensive before the 73-year-old ex-president fled to Kenya. There, he settled briefly, before being forced to seek refuge in Nigeria, thanks to pressure against the Kenyan government by Somali opposition groups. He died of a heart attack in January 1995.

The final ouster of the Siad Barre regime did not, ultimately, offer much relief for the Somali people, and nor did it precipitate peace and the emergence of a democratic government. Quite the opposite in fact. Clan unity fractured the moment that the remnants of Siad Barre's army ceased to be a threat, and the strongmen and warlords turned on one another in an effort to gain a permanent power foothold at a national level.

Mohammed Farah Aidid made the not unreasonable assumption that he, as the principal military leader and tactician of the revolution, would be poised to lead the country. However, effective control remained, in the interim, with individual insurgent leaders in the regions, tending towards a negative polarity that resisted any civil and non-governmental efforts towards the establishment of a central authority. Moreover, fighting among the clans for local and regional control did much to exacerbate the conditions of famine that were, by then, being acutely felt throughout the south of the country and, to a lesser but growing extent, elsewhere. On 17 May 1991, the north seceded along the geographic lines of the old British Somaliland, declaring its independence as the Somaliland Republic. This secession has never been recognized, notwithstanding that the new republic remained insulated somewhat from the grave insecurity afflicting the south, and has remained largely peaceful and subject to central authority, as the south has steadily descended into utter anarchy.

The final, awful act of a bloody tragedy played out in the Battle for Mogadishu. The two principal USC leaders, Aidid and Ali Mahdi Mohamed, the latter a fellow Hawiye of the Abgaal clan who had united with Aidid to confront Siad Barre, turned against each other, each questing for national power, recognizing also that control of Mogadishu was key to control of the country. As 1991 drew to an end, both sides occupied quarters of the capital and girded for a final confrontation. Insecurity was rife and tension in the city palpable as the streets came under the sway of armed and belligerent youths untroubled by authority and beyond the control of either leader. Fighting broke out in September 1991, continuing until February 1992, resulting in tens of thousands of deaths and effectively destroying a city that lay under constant and random artillery bombardment for several months. With an absolute and, at times, utterly incomprehensible indifference to human life, and the mass suffering of the wider population, the struggle continued. The by-now familiar images of the ruined boulevards of a once elegant city began to settle into the global consciousness, as this human atrocity played out on television screens worldwide. Seeping into the reportage was equally stark imagery of medieval human suffering on the fringes of cities, and in the deep hinterland, as the inevitable result of failed harvest and mass starvation began to seriously grip the countryside. The United Nations, which had long fled the conflict, left only a handful of smaller agencies and relief organizations battling against astronomical odds to feed an exploding population of starving people.

Effective relief was impossible. Insecurity was absolute. In the United Nations a strange lethargy affected the bureaucracy as the outgoing secretary-general, Javier Pérez de Cuéllar, prepared to hand over to recently appointed Boutros Boutros-Ghali, perhaps the worst possible choice of UN secretary-general that could have been made under the circumstance. Mohammed Farah Aidid suffered from a deep personal enmity towards Boutros-Ghali for a variety of reasons, not least his belief that as Egyptian minister of state for foreign affairs, Boutros-Ghali had been instrumental in Egypt's support of Siad Barre. This feeling appeared to have been wholly reciprocated by Boutros-Ghali.

The situation in Somalia, meanwhile, was, by the end of 1992, almost incomprehensibly dire, demanding world attention and forcing a global leadership, reluctant to involve itself militarily in Africa, to do something, and do something quickly.

CHAPTER ONE: THE UNITED NATIONS IN SOMALIA

Disarmament was excluded from the mission because it was neither realistically achievable nor a prerequisite or the core mission of providing a secure environment for relief operations
- General Joseph P. Hoar

The United Nations fumbled the Somalia issue, highlighting more or less from the outset inherent deficiencies in the UN structure – highly bureaucratized, personality-driven and excessively procedure-dependent – as well as uncertainties within the organization as a whole as to how to tackle events such as Somalia against a backdrop of the New World Order. It also highlighted some of the unique and unexpected problems associated with peacekeeping, and peacemaking, in regions such as Africa, where the normal tenets of humanitarianism appeared to carry absolutely no currency. It was then, as it remains today, a source of astonishment, expressed in countless UN and independent academic analyses of the experience, that the Somalis themselves proved to be the defining obstacle in attempting to provide crisis-relief to Somalia. Grassroots extortion and banditry probably dominated the catalogue of difficulties experienced by relief organizations, but, qualitatively, it was the politicization of food aid and the difficulty of dealing with a constantly evolving lattice work of clan alliances and enmities that underwrote most of the significant failures. On a certain level, food aid was simply stolen by anyone with opportunity to do so and, on another, it was claimed by individual clans and clan alliances to the detriment of others. With security provided, in many cases, by the Somalis themselves, there was almost no control over where the food ended up once it had been passed into, or had been expropriated by, Somali hands. Humanitarian organizations were forced to deal with Somali gunmen more or less on their own terms. Militia gangs were contracted as 'technical' staff, but were essentially operating protection rackets, often stealing the shipments they were employed to protect and defining their own terms of employment through armed threat.

Rarely did a food shipment find its way into the hands of the starving, highlighting, once again, the incomprehensible prioritization of local clan politics over any attempts to respond to a calamitous general misfortune, and, moreover, to actively prevent others from effectively doing so.

The net result was a crisis of mind-haunting human suffering. Images of crisis dominated foreign newsreels, and, if this failed to wrench at the consciences of the dominant Somali clans, it certainly did motivate the world at large. International anguish was expressed through rolling debates and conferences held under the general aegis of the UN Security Council, the Organization of African Unity, the League of Arab States and the Organization of the Islamic Conference; with a chorus of political lobbies, NGOs, religious groups and relief organizations added urgency to a general call for emergency action in Somalia.

The first substantive UN move in the region was the adopting of Security Council Resolution 797, which endorsed Secretary-General Boutros Boutros-Ghali's call for an emergency airlift of food into the Triangle of Death to avert the very worst of the disaster. In support of this, US president, George Bush, authorized a US airlift – Operation Provide Relief – which utilized ten USAF and US Air National Guard Lockheed C-130 Hercules transports to air deliver some 48,000 tons of emergency food aid. Additional Canadian air assets were deployed under the separate but concurrent Operation Deliverance. A number of private chartered aircraft were used too. The operation was launched from Mombasa airport during August 1992, continuing until February 1993 when it was superseded by Operation Restore Hope.

The operation was commanded by Marine brigadier-general, Frank Libutti, and was protected by troops of the 2nd Battalion 5th Special Forces Group (Airborne). These were deployed to Kenya, from where they operated as an airborne reaction force. Their platform was a C-130 that circled over Somali airstrips during the delivery of relief supplies, having on board two light desert-mobility vehicles. In addition, Special Operations Force medics and ground observers accompanied most relief flights into many of the more remote airstrips throughout southern Somalia to conduct general area assessments.

The airlift preceded other, more coordinated UN actions, but inasmuch as it was intended as shock treatment to bypass the difficulties presented by militia control of ports and road networks, it was only partially successful. Militia groups simply took control of airports and landing zones, demanding, in addition to landing fees, anything else that could be profitably extorted from organizations attempting to coordinate shipments on the ground. It very quickly became evident that, notwithstanding some damping down of the crisis, airlifts alone would not be able to significantly impact the situation on the ground. Statistics indicated a gradual worsening of the situation, once again largely attributable to insecurity, which tended to reinforce the fact that little on the ground was possible without attention being given to some sort of robust military response. Local representatives of the Office of Foreign Disaster Assistance even briefly pondered the possibility of flooding Somalia with food to the extent that commodity prices would collapse and looting would no longer be profitable.

Much of the difficultly lay in a singular lack of enthusiasm on the part of the world community for armed intervention. For example, the force complement of a proposed UNOSOM,

Somalis sit in the sun as they wait for food provided during Operation Provide Relief. This was one of many sights taken in by a congressional fact-finding delegation. The delegates, directed by John Lewis and Bill Emerson, toured several humanitarian relief sites to determine the impact of US aid in the besieged country.

Somalis working the fields near Kismayo.

Air Force Reserve units participated in Operation Provide Relief/Restore Hope, a massive airlift of food and medical supplies to millions of starving Somalis. Eighteen Air National Guard and Air Force Reserve C-130s flew 20 missions a day from Moi International Airport (Mombasa, to war-torn Somalia.

or United Nations Operation in Somalia, was authorized at 500 men, in this case drawn from elements of the Pakistani Army who would be operating under a limited mandate to secure the port, safeguard food shipments to and from the airport and to escort food convoys. The Pakistani battalion was preceded by an advance party of 50 United Nations observers, drawn from a variety of countries, also led by a Pakistani brigadier.

Typically abstruse UN rules of engagement, plus a constraining chain of command, effectively hobbled the Pakistani contingent when it arrived, confining it to camp at the airport, where soldiers were daily ignored and ridiculed by armed looters.

As Operation Provide Relief continued to shuttle food into the country in a cost-prohibitive and narrowly focused programme to provide the most basic emergency relief, without artillery, air support or heavy weapons the Pakistanis were incapable of achieving anything at all to advance this. An additional 3,000 troops approved for the mission upset the delicate diplomatic balance within Somalia, and ultimately never arrived.

In December 1992, the UN accepted a US offer of 30,000 troops that would form the bulk of a combined UN intervention force. This was offered as a consequence of both a renewed US sense of mission in a post-Cold War world and the stark clarity of UN paralysis. It was well received on an official level at the UN, for clearly something had to be done, and, alone, the UN was incapable of doing it. The formalities were a little more difficult, but after a certain amount of hand-wringing over the regulatory minutiae, on 3 December 1992, the UN Security Council adopted Resolution 794, authorizing the formation of the United Task Force (UNITAF) for the purpose of creating a secure environment for the provision of humanitarian services to the population of Somalia. Key to this was the invocation of Chapter VII of the UN Charter authorizing the use of force for the purpose of peace enforcement, thus sidestepping complicated sovereignty issues in a situation whereby neither of the belligerents in a conflict had specifically requested UN intervention or, in the case of Somalia, where no recognized government existed to formally make that request.

On 4 December 1992, US president, George Bush, appeared before the nation in a television broadcast to announce to the American people and the world that the United States would be contributing 28,000 troops to Somalia at the head of a US-led multinational force to be codenamed Operation Restore Hope. Other contributing forces included Australia, Bangladesh, Belgium, Botswana, Canada, Egypt, France, Germany, Greece, India, Republic of Ireland, Italy, Kuwait, Morocco, New Zealand, Nigeria, Norway, Pakistan, Saudi Arabia, Spain, Sweden, Tunisia, Turkey, United Arab Emirates, the United Kingdom and Zimbabwe.

CHAPTER TWO: UNITED TASK FORCE (UNITAF)

There does not appear to be any particular centre of gravity, no single leader or faction or army whose defeat will bring stability
– Central Command

On the evening of 6 December 1992, a team of US Navy Seals slipped into the surf surrounding Mogadishu to conduct a detailed hydrographic reconnaissance ahead of a Marine amphibious assault scheduled to be launched within 48 hours. A large US Navy flotilla waited in readiness in the waters of southern Somalia. This was the Tripoli Amphibious Ready Group, comprising the USS *Tripoli* (LPH 10), USS *Juneau* (LPD 10) and USS *Rushmore* (LSD 47), and collectively carrying the men and equipment earmarked to spearhead the massive military and civil undertaking that would be Operation Restore Hope. Under the slough of arcane political manoeuvring that had been swilling back and forth between the White House and the United Nations, military planners had been quietly and diligently working to assemble the complex framework of a task force for insertion into what was arguably one of the most inhospitable, dysfunctional corners of Africa.* Although formal

* In US military parlance, the term most often applied is an 'austere' operational environment.

Lieutenant-General Robert B. Johnston, US Marine Corps

General Joseph P. Hoar, CENTCOM commander

An aerial view of the port of Mogadishu. Three cargo ships, large-, medium- and small-sized vessels, are moored at the docks. A tugboat is heading out of the port. A US Marine UH-1N 'Huey' helicopter flies left to right at the right of the frame. The port played an important role in the support of Operation Restore Hope.

US Army troops from the 10th Mountain Division conducting a nighttime sweep for weapons in the small Somali village of Afgooye.

notification of the pending operation had only been handed down to CENTCOM on 2 December, 1992, notification had been given several weeks earlier than that to Lieutenant-General Robert B. Johnston, commanding general of 1 Marine Expeditionary Force (1MEF), in respect of the fact that 1MEF was earmarked to assume headquarters responsibility for what would initially be termed Joint Task Force (JTF) Somalia, the military force charged with undertaking Operation Restore Hope.

Somalia, it must be remembered, remained within the CENTCOM area of operation, which placed it under the overall oversight of General Joseph Hoar. Johnston was recognized as a highly capable, intuitive and charismatic commander. He had served during Operation Desert Storm as Chief of Staff to General Norman Schwarzkopf, prior to which his experience had been as a senior officer during the early phases of US peacekeeping operations in Beirut, dealing with a number of political factions, including the Palestinian Liberation Organization (PLO).

Once activated, JTF Somalia would enjoy operational control of all participating forces, effectively placing the entire operation under US command and control. Most of the force complement, of course, would be US in origin, with the two principal ground combat formations being 1 Marine Expeditionary Division and the army's 10th Mountain Division. These would be known as Marine Force Somalia, or MARFOR, and Army Force Somalia, or ARFOR. Collectively these were commanded by 1st Marine Division commander, Major-General Charles B. Wilhelm.

MARFOR comprised a total of 16,200 personnel, including four infantry battalions, one artillery battalion, one tank battalion, one amtrack battalion and one light armoured vehicle battalion. ARFOR, commanded by Major-General Steven L. Arnold, totalled 10,200 men, arranged into three light infantry battalions and one artillery battalion. Arnold did not arrive in the theatre until 22 December 1992. The initial beach-landing would be undertaken by one of the Marine Expeditionary Force's organic units, the 15th Marine Expeditionary Unit (MEU), commanded by Colonel Gregory S. Newbold, which was already embarked in the Western Pacific and was thus poised to arrive in the waters off Somalia with a minimum of pre-preparation.

The ground combat element would be formed around the 2nd Battalion 9th Marines, reinforced by a light armoured infantry platoon, a combat engineer platoon, a platoon of amphibious assault vehicles and a battery of artillery in direct support.

The air combat element was no less formidable. Nicknamed 'the Knightriders', the Marine Medium Helicopter Squadron (Composite) 164 was powered by an range of helicopters: Boeing CH-46E Sea Knights, Sikorsky CH-53E Sea Stallions, Bell AH-1W Super Cobras, and Bell UH-1N Iroquois 'Hueys'. Combat service support was provided by MEU Service Support Group 15.

The MEU was embarked on the three ships, comprising Amphibious Squadron 3, commanded by Captain John W. Preston, and including one of the ships of Maritime Prepositioning Squadron 3, the MV *1st Lt Jack Lummus* (T-AK 3011), which was assigned to the amphibious squadron for the purpose of providing

USS *Ranger* (CV 61)

USS *Valley Forge* (CG 50)

USS *Kincaid* (DD 965)

additional equipment and support to the MEU.

The bulk of naval and air support was also provided by the United States, with Naval Forces Somalia being somewhat hastily established from task forces in the Central Command area of operations, or from assets that could be ordered into the area reasonably quickly. Principal among these was the Ranger carrier battle group, consisting of the aircraft carriers USS *Ranger* (CV 61) and USS *Valley Forge* (CG 50) and the destroyer USS *Kincaid* (DD 965). Joining these forces would be the ships of Maritime Prepositioning Squadron 2, consisting of MV *1st Lt Alex Bonnyman* (T-AK 3003), MV *Pvt Franklin J. Phillips* (T-AK 3004) and MV *PFC James Anderson Jr* (T-AK 3002). Throughout the operation, additional squadrons, groups and ships of the navies of the United States and various coalition partners would enter the area of operations and become part of Naval Forces Somalia.

Air Force Somalia was arguably the most important single component, bearing in mind that, although naval shipping would handle the heavy lifting, most of the personnel and lighter equipment complements would be delivered to the theatre by air. Five hundred individuals would be involved directly in the air operation, with many thousands of others indirectly involved at various points along the air bridge.

Special Operation Forces – primarily liaison – and Support Command – mainly logistic – were additional, although much smaller components. Both, however, were extremely important: in the case of Special Operations to coordinate between various key contributing forces, and in the case of Support Command to expedite the introduction of just about everything necessary to conduct the operation in an absence of any meaningful infrastructure on the ground.

Having made this point, it would be untrue to suggest that Somali national infrastructure had completely broken down. Port facilities in Mogadishu and Kismayo were both usable, but required upgrading for the volume of anticipated traffic. The militarization of the country under Siad Barre, in combination with the extensive military infrastructure created by the Italians prior to the Second World War, had left a residue of some 40 usable air facilities. UNITAF operations required, in the main, for an airfield to be C-130-capable as a minimum, and of the existing airfields available, only ten met this standard. Six of the ten could also handle US C-141 Starlifters, although the massive C-5 Galaxy military transport aircraft could land only at Mogadishu and Berbera. A national road system, comprising some 18,000 kilometres of roadway, was broadly serviceable if somewhat depleted from a lack of maintenance. The nation was without a railway system.

In the absence of reliable intelligence prior to the launch of the operation, estimates of what UNITAF would be confronting in

The abandoned Mogadishu street known as the 'Green Line', the dividing line between north and south of the city, and the warring clans. Foliage has grown up along the sidewalks and a burned-out car can be seen in the centre of the frame. Members of the clans have torn down the roadblocks along the line in a show of unity.

The Somali village of Bardera. Vehicles are seen leaving on a dirt road that leads out of the town. The Botswana Defence Force provides security for the humanitarian relief groups that are distributing food to the townspeople.

pure military terms were vague. According to General Hoar:

> Over all, the security environment throughout Somalia is volatile. The situation may deteriorate further because there is no centralized governmental control of Somali factions.

His security assessment continued as follows:

Mogadishu: The security situation in Mogadishu remains uncertain. Large numbers of armed forces (estimated 5,000–10,000 aligned under General [Mohamed Farah Hassan] Aidid and estimated 5,000–6,000 aligned under interim president [Ali Mahdi Mohamed]) roam the city with the two opposing leaders ... exercising little control over their activities. While Ali Mahdi appears to welcome UN presence and assistance in Somalia, General Aidid opposes such presence and has threatened the 500-man Pakistani force and impeded that unit from securing the port and airfield in Mogadishu. Further, General Aidid has publicly stated that he will oppose any further introduction of UN forces into Mogadishu.

Kismayo: The security situation in Kismayo is uncertain, but less volatile than Mogadishu. Factional fighting occurs frequently and the general population is known to be armed. Random shootings and violent incidents are frequent. The two factions claiming this area have formed a loose alliance with about 3,000 troops, many of whom were former Somali National Army soldiers, reasonably well-trained and experienced with weapons. The apparent leader, Colonel [Ahmed Omar] Jess, appears to be minimizing his ties with General Aidid and has indicated a willingness to have a UN contingent deploy to Kismayo.

Key Assumptions: The primary threat to security will be armed lawlessness and armed looters.[4]

A fact of military operations involving divergent cultures is the difficulty of intelligence. Colonial powers in the past confronted this problem to varying degrees, and over several decades of occupation, but never did they absolutely succeed in piercing the cultural divide that separated white from black. Native militias, native police forces and elaborate pseudo operations were all devices used to penetrate local guerrilla and insurgent networks during the various wars of liberation fought by the French, British and Portuguese. In an environment such as Somalia, however, with tight-knit clan affiliations dominating the social landscape, and the limited timeframes of UN and other operations, the likelihood of a widespread and reliable intelligence network developing quickly enough to be useful, was highly unlikely. Clan enmities offered some potential to exploit localized situations, and this would prove key in later operations but, on a wider scale, intelligence remained a key difficulty.

A late-model Isuzu dump truck loaded with Somali men. One man rides on the right front fender, while two others ride on the top of the truck's cab. They are from the village of Maleel and are arriving at a landing zone where bags of wheat are being delivered.

A variable Omni-Range meteorological navigational aids system, utilizing an AN/FRN-44 VOR Site Survey van with a VHF Omni-Range radio. The site was set up by the 485th Engineering Installation Group, Griffiss, Air Force Base, New York. The purpose of the vans was to help civilian aircraft navigate into Mogadishu airport.

Technology was employed to achieve basic operational intelligence for the deployment of UNITAF, utilizing a wide range of intelligence systems which were deployed, in some instances, for the first time. Night-vision devices, ground surveillance radars, tactical air reconnaissance and unmanned aerial vehicles were all utilized to accumulate tactical intelligence and early warning information. However, it is Human Intelligence, HUMINT in the complex military parlance of the United States, that is the low-tech catalyst for really understanding what is afoot at the grassroots level of insurgent organization. Good Human Intelligence is irreplaceable in a low-intensity conflict. The CIA was active in Somalia, as it had been for some time, and the cultivation of intelligence assets in the militia community was ongoing, and it would be this that would account for the basic intelligence received which would later precipitate the dramatic events of 3 October 1993. The best source of HUMINT, however, was then, and remains, boots on the ground. A comprehensive situational awareness was maintained by adjusting patrol tactics and intelligence requirements to make best use of the eyes and ears of the soldiers or marines in the field.

To centralize and collate this information in an operational environment lacking the most basic communications infrastructure, challenged even the proven capacity of the US armed forces to organize on a massive scale. The key lay in satellite communications and, to provide a focal point for information dissemination, CENTCOM established an Intelligence Support Element (ISE), which was staffed solely by US personnel. This quickly became the most important intelligence support asset to UNOSOM, with only a minor complication in a multi-national context insofar as US law that expressly forbids dissemination of intelligence through any channel over which there is anything other than US control. There was also the question of sensitive US intelligence sources and methods being compromised, which was dealt with by the issuing of guidelines that limited the giving out of information relating to targets and operational security, while generally permitting the flow of timely intelligence to the coalition. US officers serving in UNOSOM Force Command Staff normally filtered information developed by the ISE in support of specific operations, with commander of the US forces in Somalia, Major-General Montgomery, usually making the final judgement on what would be generally made available. In all cases, though, UN force commander, Lieutenant-General Cevik Bir, was kept fully apprised of the overall US intelligence picture as it related to his area of operations.

Enemy force levels were obviously extremely difficult to ascertain, with personnel being particularly difficult to pin down, thanks to the general fluidity of service within individual militias, and the fact that a majority of adult males in the country were in one way or another armed and aligned.

Aidid's United Somali Congress (USC) was estimated at approximately 20,000 fighters, with Ali Mahdi's chapter of the organization thought to number upward of 15,000 militiamen, with possibly as many as 30,000 under arms. Both were known to have significant weapons stockpiles, including mixed artillery, tanks, armoured personnel carriers and, of course, the ubiquitous 'technicals.'

In the south, in and around the port of Kismayo, the two principal factions of the Somali National Front (SNF), under Mohamed Said Hirsi, known also as General Morgan, and the rival Somali Patriotic Movement (SPM), under Colonel Omar Jess, fielded a force of, respectively, 9,000 men and 15,000 men, the former having among his fighters many trained men of the former national army.[5]

The combined numerical advantage of the various Somali militias was tempered by a number of significant operational disadvantages. Not least of these was the disunited nature of the Somali clans. This should not imply that each could not individually assume an aggressive posture towards coalition forces, but simply that it was extremely unlikely that this would take place with any broad coordination. Other disadvantages identifiable among the Somali factions were a general lack of training and discipline among the militias, a questionable ability to use and maintain the sophisticated weapons systems that had been acquired, and the fact that many fighters were young and, moreover, were almost universally under the influence of a local narcotic plant name *khat*.

At this point, a brief examination of khat in respect of how it influenced the mood and general combat willingness of Somali fighters would be useful. Grown throughout the Horn of Africa and the Arabian Peninsular, khat, known variously as Arabian tea, *qat*, *gat*, or *miraa*, is a green leaf plant, the chewing of which induces a mild sense of euphoria combined with the stimulant properties of hyper-alertness, talkativeness and general loss of appetite. Its traditional value has been as a social catalyst, not unlike alcohol, that offers a generally positive initial mood-enhancement, followed, after several hours, by emotional depletion, instability, irritability and listlessness. Although not dissimilar in general pharmacological action to coffee, also popular in the region, the use of khat goes back much further, and certainly it remains in generally wider use as an indispensible social medium in a largely alcohol-free environment.

The question of the addictive qualities of khat remains an open debate, but it can be surmised by the extent to which the substance has become embedded in the day-to-day life of the region, and in expatriate communities worldwide, that some higher level of dependency is experienced by khat users that tends to prompt addictive responses. Journalist Jonathan Stevenson, commenting in his book, *Losing Mogadishu*, relates an incident that speaks volumes of the importance of khat in the lives of the militiamen of Somalia. 'In September [1992] a Somali employee of a French relief agency, who was paid half in food, instead of all in cash, detained several expatriate doctors and nurses in an operating theatre with an unpinned hand grenade until he got his way. Food couldn't buy khat.'[6]

The widespread use of khat emerged as a factor in the conduct of this and future operations in Somalia, influencing enemy battlefield performance to the extent that the ebb and flow of aggression and displays of courage and bravado could be timed, fairly accurately, to the daily sequence of morning ingestion, midday lethargy and evening lulls. It also tended to influence the view that was generated among non-Islamic servicemen of the Somalis in general, and Somali militiamen in particular. The first UN troop contingent in Somalia was Pakistani, and, perhaps with Islam in common, and with surprisingly comprehensive pre-preparation, Pakistani commanders and troops tended to view the Somalis with more appreciation and respect than the average western soldier was wont. Khat was viewed by US commanders, generally, as an illegal drug, and would have been subject to seizure had anyone possessed the stomach to rock the local boat to that extent; but, at the very least, it reinforced a view rather cynically expressed by UNICEF's local representative, Mark Stirling, in a January 1993 interview, stating that Somalis in general presented themselves as khat-chewing thugs lying under a long-hauler.*

There was nothing present in the many briefs circulating prior to deployment that offered any prospect of a real military challenge. Nonetheless, the MEU and the special force elements earmarked to spearhead the landing prepared for the assault could hardly have expected to encounter a large body of the international press corps waiting for them on the beach as they emerged from the surf in the predawn darkness in full combat mode. The startling reception of flashing cameras and milling journalists briefly paused forward momentum, but only briefly, and with the smooth efficiency of arguably the best-trained soldiers in the world, the Marines and SEALs came ashore. The US Navy SEALs swam in from offshore while 170 Marines in 18 Zodiac-type assault craft landed at various points along the beach.

Colonel Gregory S. Newbold had emphasized speed and force in the matter of achieving what was expected to be a highly observed if unopposed landing. This was certainly accomplished. As the reconnaissance teams moved inland to secure the port and the airport, the majority of the landing force followed soon afterward in a variety of amphibious assault vehicles, helicopters and air-cushioned landing craft (hovercraft).

Colonel Newbold was able to declare the airport and port facilities secure at 11h45, by which time, the MV *1st Lt Jack Lummus* was already entering Mogadishu port to begin unloading heavy equipment, while, a few minutes later, the first air force Lockheed C-141 carrying members of the task force headquarters

* Mark Stirling, in fact, presented this comment in the singular, and in reference to the negative image generated by the superficial efforts taken by the US military to engender understanding of Somali culture: 'a khat-chewing thug lying under a long-hauler'. The comment was made at the UNICEF headquarters in Mogadishu on 9 January 1993, and is reproduced by Jonathan Stevenson in his 1995 book, *Losing Mogadishu*.

was touching down at the airport. From there, the Marines quickly moved into the city to secure the US embassy chancery building within the US embassy compound, which was earmarked for the Joint Task Force headquarters. By the end of day one, all objectives had been achieved and a forward operations command post established at the airport.

For the remainder of the day, the airport saw steady traffic as incoming coalition forces quickly began to arrive. The first of these was a company of the 2nd French Foreign Legion Parachute Regiment – *2e Régiment Étranger de Parachutistes* – flying in from their base in Djibouti. The men of this elite regiment came

United States Air Force Lockheed C-141A Starlifter

A US Marine, holding an M16A2 rifle, guards seven Somali nationals sitting on the ground next to a Somali BTR-60PB. The Somalis were detained during an early morning raid on General Aidid's weapons cantonment.

immediately under US operational control and, in fact, fired the first shots of the campaign when a vehicle containing nine Somalis ran a checkpoint manned by the legionnaires, who promptly opened fire, killing two and wounding seven. The incident provoked a certain amount of anxiety over the question of rules of engagement (RoE), and while it was informally agreed that the French had been somewhat hasty in engaging the fleeing vehicle, the situation could be deemed to have posed a threat to coalition forces, and was thus declared a legitimate target. UNITAF RoEs listed four basic 'nos': no 'technicals', no banditry, no roadblocks and no visible weapons.

The first direct attacks on UNITAF members in fact occurred on 12 December when three aircraft of Marine Medium Helicopter Squadron 164 were fired upon. A UH-1N Huey received damage to its rotors. In a second incident attack helicopters returned fire destroying two 'technicals' and damaging one armoured personnel carrier. The only fire to be registered during the preliminary days of the operation was sporadic, but ongoing sniper fire, particularly around the port area, that was neither focused nor accurate, but, nonetheless, which caused a certain amount of irritation. An old prison complex overlooked the port from where gunmen were able to direct fire into the port area.

As incoming Marine units occupied and secured positions in Mogadishu, the 15th MEU mounted an airborne assault on the abandoned Soviet air facility in the town of Bale-Dogle, some 50 kilometres north of Mogadishu, in order to handle the overflow of air traffic from Mogadishu airport. At 10,000 feet, Bale-Dogle ranks as the second-longest runway in Africa. The Marines were supported by elements of the Marine Medium Helicopter Squadron 164, and were relieved soon afterwards by 10th Mountain Division troops from Company A, 2nd Battalion, 87th Infantry. The most dangerous aspect of the operation was the presence, less than a kilometre from the terminal, of a bunker containing undetonated Soviet bombs and other ordnance in such dangerous levels of heat that, at some stage, a combustion point would almost inevitably have been reached.

General Johnston arrived in Mogadishu on 10 December, the day after the initial assault, and was immediately absorbed in the minutiae of the massive operation. For the first few days of the active operation, he was engaged in the preliminary tasks of establishing contacts with key individuals already operational in the capital, occupied mostly with managing the ongoing arrivals of large numbers of US and coalition troops.

Perhaps the main priority Johnston faced was the establishment of his Joint Task Force headquarters at the US Embassy Chancery building, recently secured by the MEU. Before this could be done, the building and surrounds required significant cleaning up and renovating. Since the evacuation of embassy staff a year earlier, the building had been reduced to its skeletal exterior, with every removable fixture looted and the compound clogged with refuse and a few mummified corpses. Once this unpleasant task had been completed, the US flag was once again raised in the embassy compound, the same flag that had flown over the Marine barracks in Beirut, which had been retrieved in the aftermath of the 1983 bomb blast that killed 299 American and French servicemen.

Similarly, the main port at Mogadishu required extensive rehabilitation before it would be capable of receiving the quantity of shipping that was beginning to converge on the theatre. The maritime prepositioning ship, MV *1st LT Jack Lummus*, stood ready for unloading, which was scheduled to take four days, and which quickly expedited the dispersal of vital equipment to the troops assembling on the ground. A maritime prepositioning force squadron typically contains enough equipment and supplies for a Marine brigade of 16,000 men.

Malaysian UN peacekeeping soldiers stand in formation to practise drill inside their headquarters located near the airport in Mogadishu. They all carry British-made 7.62mm Enfield L1A1 rifles.

An unidentified Somali truck backs up to the open rear entrance of a US Air Force C-130 Hercules cargo plane.

A massive amount of general clearance and demolition also took place, eventually opening up some 54 acres of area as an initial staging point, followed over the course of the next few months by the construction of new warehouses, barracks and galleys, amounting to an enormous infrastructural project as a collateral benefit of the overall operation. By the end of December, with a combination of backlogged humanitarian and military supplies, Mogadishu had grown to be one of the busiest ports in Africa.

Humanitarian organizations, perhaps in some respects missing the point, were quite often angrily vocal about the priority given to military shipping in the queues for unloading. Over 35 days, 48 military ships were offloaded of 114,000 tons of cargo, including 6,668 vehicles, 96 helicopters, over 5 million gallons of fuel and 832,000 gallons of water. During the same period 14 non-military cargo vessels unloaded 40,000 tons of grain. By mid-December, Johnston was sending shipments of heavy weapons systems back without unloading them. The consensus at that time was that the situation did not warrant heavy operational equipment.

In respect of the fact that this was only partially a military operation, Johnston was very quickly required to attend to certain key diplomatic stepping stones necessary to get the larger operation off the ground. A certain amount of institutionalized impatience was expressed as, with absolute professionalism, Johnston allowed the foundation of the operation, in terms of force build-up and general provisions for security and command and control, to be fully established before he would contemplate the commencement of Phase Two. In the meanwhile, he would be introduced to a man who would guide him through the turbulent diplomatic waters of Somalia, as he attempted to present both the stern and the yielding faces of what was now being referred to UNITAF, or United Task Force.

Veteran US diplomat, Robert Oakley, had been appointed by President George Bush as his special representative in Somalia, a man uniquely qualified to embrace the almost impossible demands of reconciling each opposing faction

President Bush rides in a Humvee with General H. Norman Schwarzkopf during a visit to troops in Saudi Arabia.

United Nations Indian Army T-72 main battle tanks in the Belgian compound at Kismayo.

leader to the imminent arrival of UNITAF – which he succeeded in doing – but, thereafter, to ensure that each step taken by the military in pursuit of the operational objectives was covered by prior diplomatic preparation, in order to minimize the risk of misunderstanding, misconstruction or simple opportunism in the face of an opaque situation.

Oakley, incidentally, was returning to familiar ground when ordered to Mogadishu. He was a seasoned diplomat, having been in the past US ambassador to Pakistan, Zaire and Somalia. His brief on this occasion was to oversee and coordinate all US civilian activities in Somalia, to provide political advice to UNITAF, to act as liaison to the local UN representative, Iraqi diplomat Ismat T. Kittani, and to work closely with the NGO community to jump-start large-scale relief operations. Some 50 separate relief organizations were operational in Somalia. Johnston, on the other hand, was charged to provide what security was necessary for the successful completion of this task.

Ismat T. Kittani, it is worth pointing out, had been on the scene for some time, and had proved to be less than a comfortable fit in Somalia. This was perhaps because he was something of a UN stereotype, inasmuch as he appeared to place more importance on the UN as a diplomatic force in Somalia than it deserved, and certainly an excess of importance in himself as its representative. This, bearing in mind the visceral antipathy towards the organization expressed by many important Somalis, could hardly have failed to alienate him. Oakley, on the other hand, represented the United States, a more widely respected international presence in Somalia than the UN, which also happened to be backed up by a considerable military force, which, of course, the UN, in real terms, was not.

One of Johnston's first priorities was a meeting held between him, Oakley and the two principal Somali warlords – Ali Mahdi and Farah Aidid – in what was, in actual fact, something of a landmark diplomatic achievement on the part of Oakley. He was not only able to bring together such sworn enemies as the two Somali warlords round a common table – Ismat Kittani was also present, against the objections of Aidid, which Oakley could not agree to, since he had to be seen to be supportive of the UN role as the ultimate arbitrator of the situation, and nor could Aidid be seen to be getting his way – and, what is more, he was able to guide them successfully toward a ceasefire agreement, with an additional undertaking to withdraw hostile forces from the city and form a liaison committee to coordinate policy. This resulted in an ad hoc committee – the Combined Security Committee – which offered an ongoing forum for General Johnston and key members of his staff to meet regularly with Aidid, Ali Mahdi and other key clan leaders. 'You may not like the characters you have to deal with,' Johnston noted, 'but you are better able to uncover their motives and intentions if you keep a communications link open.'[7]

How much weight, in practical terms, could be applied to the liaison achieved in the Combined Security Committee is naturally open to interpretation, but such dialogue continued for the duration of Operation Restore Hope, and no major breaches were recorded.

Another key initiative was the Civil-Military Operations Centre which was set up in December 1992 for the purpose of providing a liaison platform between UNITAF and the many humanitarian relief organizations (HROs) operating in the country, some 50 at the height of the relief effort. Liaison officers from all the major military contingents, alongside the US command, made use of this centre to coordinate such activities as the provision of military support for relief convoys and the assignment of pier space at, and port access to, Mogadishu harbour for processing the food and other supply deliveries for the various HROs. This role provided a vital point of contact between military and civil operations, broadening eventually to include the issuing of ID cards and maintaining a data matrix showing the status of food and relief supplies across the operational spectrum.[8]

As all this was taking place, the movement of troops and equipment into the country continued. Next to arrive in theatre was a Canadian airborne regiment battle group, followed by an initial deployment of two battalions of the Italian *Folgore* Airborne Parachute Brigade, and the San Marco Regiment, a naval infantry unit. Italian forces also enjoyed naval support from the Italian Navy's 24th Naval Group carrying heavy equipment and supplies.

Special Envoy to Somalia, Ambassador Robert Oakley, speaking to a group of Somalis over a public address system. Behind him and to the left is US Army Brigadier-General Lawson W. Magruder III, vice-commander,10th Mountain Division (Light), in Somalia as the commander of Combined Task Force Kismayo.

Johnston, incidentally, deployed the Italians with caution. Italy, the erstwhile colonizing power in Somalia, carried a potentially difficult stigma that, although practically irrelevant, was available for abuse by various warlords looking for issues to complicate the deployment. Similar complaints were heard against the Belgians during the occupation of Kismayo, who had colonized Zaire/Congo, and who could hardly have projected any particularly damaging symbolism in Somalia.

Next came the 1st Battalion, 1st Royal Australian Regiment, followed by a Turkish task force configured around an existing mechanized infantry company, the 1st Company, 1st Battalion, 28th Mechanized Brigade, with an additional quartermaster platoon, a transport platoon, a signal section, a medical section and an engineer section. These were introduced directly into the theatre by the Turkish Navy.

A number of other contingents formed the bricks of the international coalition, but not necessarily the mortar. It is a fact of UN international military operations that the majority of contributing nations are invited to participate simply to enhance the international flavour of operations, and most comply on the understanding that duty with the United Nations pays a portion of their defence budgets. Equipment considered standard, even basic in most western armies, are often absent from the inventories of many developing world armies. The responsibility then falls on the UN commander to make up the shortfalls, which, in this case, was usually through US stocks, which left many of these forces in theatre occupying a symbolic role and relegated to non-essential patrolling, security and garrison duties.

With the principal forces in place, and with the general ongoing movement of troops from various contributing nations into the country, Johnston, in due course, began to turn his attention to Phase II of the operation, concluding Phase I by securing the settlement of Baidoa. To achieve this, Task Force Hope was formed from a combination of the French 2nd Foreign Legion Parachute Regiment, elements of the French Special Operations Command, the 13th Foreign Legion Demi-Brigade and 15th MEU. On 15 December, six days after the first landing, the assembled task force left Mogadishu overland and quickly secured the extensive Baidoa airfield through a combined heliborne and ground movement. No opposition was registered and relief convoys began to move into the town that afternoon. French troops and Marines quickly established security posts, before deploying patrols through the town. Note was taken of large numbers of passive but heavily armed men who chanced, on 18 December, to fire on members of Task Force Hope from within a compound, which was then quickly surrounded, entered and all arms confiscated. This prompt and clinical action more or less set the tone for any future response to displays of aggression, which, thereafter, did not occur.

The Baidoa operation successfully brought Phase I of Operation *Restore Hope* to a close, providing a framework for the ongoing operation, and leading smoothly into Phase II. The first major operation of Phase II was to secure the port of Kismayo, which, although not specifically a famine-affected area, offered key port facilities to launch operations into the southern, and most affected regions of the country, and also to cope with some of the shipping congestion in Mogadishu. Another factor was the existence of air

A German soldier hands out candy to Somali children in Beledweyne.

facilities of appropriate size situated just outside the city.

Belgian forces were earmarked to spearhead the occupation of the city. The landing force comprised Company G, 2nd Battalion, 9th Marines supporting two platoons of Belgian paratroopers. The amphibious task force comprised *Juneau* and the *Rushmore* from the US Navy, and the French ship, PS *Dupleix*, an anti-submarine-warfare guided-missile destroyer. US Navy SEALs performed the preliminary reconnaissance, before, on the morning of 20 December, the Marine AAVs came ashore, closely followed by the Belgians in air-cushioned landing craft and helicopters. No opposition was registered and control came ashore within a few hours. US Navy captain, John Peterson, commanding the amphibious task force, and Belgian officer, Lieutenant-Colonel Marc Jacqmin, commanding the landing forces, immediately made their way into the city centre under heavy security to meet with the local warlord, Colonel Jess. Jess, notwithstanding some token grumbling about the presence of Belgians in Kismayo, quickly submitted to the inevitable. Belgian reinforcement arrived, releasing the Marine company from tactical control, which then withdrew from Kismayo, leaving 550 Belgian troops in control of the city.

The successful operation to secure Baidoa provided a template for further operations, with the next objective being Bardera, epicentre of the Triangle of Death. Located on the banks of the Juba River, Bardera had last seen large-scale foreign troop manoeuvres during the Second World War as British and Commonwealth forces pushed Italian forces back across the river towards Mogadishu, and then north up the Strada Imperiale towards a final denouement in Addis Ababa. This time, it was the US Marines in a large armoured column, comprising amphibious assault and light armoured vehicles, that arrived in the town on Christmas Day, after a long, dust-drenched and ponderous overland advance from Mogadishu and Baidoa. The column comprised advance elements of both the 3rd Amphibious Assault Battalion and the 3rd Light Armoured Infantry Battalion that had arrived in Mogadishu on 19 December. The following day, the Marines were in control of key access routes, the main river crossing over the Juba River and the city centre. From that point, coordination was established with local non-governmental organizations to facilitate the rapid movement of relief supplies to a desperate population.

A similar pattern of operations played out to secure the remaining humanitarian relief sectors. The French, with US Marine logistical support, dealt with securing the settlement of Oddur, some 260 kilometres northwest of Mogadishu, also arriving on Christmas Day, while the Italians dealt with the logistically more complicated push north from Mogadishu to the settlement of Gialalassi. Gialalassi lies 115 kilometres north of Mogadishu, and although held substantively by forces loyal to Ali Mahdi, it was also the scene of much freelance bandit activity. Early in the morning on 27 December, a large convoy left the Mogadishu port and began the difficult transit northward up the ruined remnants of the Strada Imperiale, comprising two companies of the Folgore Brigade, with headquarters, reconnaissance group, and mortar and anti-armour gun sections, accompanied by a US Army detachment and a platoon of US Military Police in

Italians recover their roller that was accidentally driven off a cliff by Somali construction workers.

A Belgian soldier performs a security check on a vehicle trying to enter the compound in Kismayo.

Belgian soldiers, part of UN forces in Somalia in support of Operation Continue Hope.

hardened Humvees.* Included also was a relief convoy of trucks containing humanitarian supplies. Occasional helicopter escorts appeared overhead as the difficult transit was negotiated, keeping a watchful eye on events until the convoy rolled into Gialalassi at 18h00 that evening.

As usual, forces proceeded directly to the airport, where a security perimeter was established for the night. The following day, platoon-sized defensive positions were established at key points in the town, after which the unloading and distribution of grain began.

The last substantive Phase II operation was to secure the city of Beledweyne, 320 kilometres north of Mogadishu, some 30 kilometres from the Ethiopian border, and the most northerly declared Humanitarian Relief Sector. The operation was assigned to 2nd Brigade (Commando Brigade) of the 10th Mountain Division. The task force would comprise the 2nd Battalion, 87th Infantry, and a battalion of the Canadian Airborne Regiment Battle Group. This time, troops were delivered to the airfield by helicopter with additional helicopter support. As soon as the airport was secure, additional troops and vehicles were landed by a Canadian C-130. In less than two days some 1,000 soldiers were in position.

Phase II of Operation Restore Hope came in about four weeks ahead of schedule, which testified to the urgency of the situation, combined with excellent planning and coordination, but perhaps, more importantly, it signalled the success of two critical elements of the operation: psychological operations – radio broadcasts, leaflet drops and the publication of a Somali-language newspaper to keep the population informed – and the diplomatic ground preparation that was conducted at every stage by Ambassador Oakley.

* UNITAF units of Army Engineers and Seabees (US Navy Construction Battalion (CB)) ultimately constructed or repaired 2,500km of roads, nine C-130-capable airfields, 85 helicopter pads, as well as multiple wells, schools and clinics.

A US Air Force public affairs representative poses with children at a Baidoa orphanage.

An ambulance backed up to the emergency room entrance of the UN field hospital, administered by Romanians, in Mogadishu.

Ferret armoured cars of the Nepalese Army, painted in the distinctive white of the United Nations, line the walls of the Napalese compound.

Key also was the fact that the Somali factions themselves had offered no resistance. On the surface a generally welcoming posture was presented but, beneath that, numerous currents imponderable to western observers were playing out, as individual warlords processed the implications of UNITAF and assessed what advantage could be gained. Militarily, the balance of power lay so steeply in favour of the coalition – compared to the threat posed by 500 politically shackled Pakistani soldiers – that no serious sabre-rattling or testing of coalition resolve took place. This was a comfortable status quo for UNITAF and, perhaps, more so the United Nations. For the warlords, however, it represented an inconvenient interlude that might present some opportunities, but that on the whole simply delayed the contest of strength that would decide the leadership complexion of the future. This was a process that would ultimately supersede any nation-building efforts by the UN, and it would certainly not be permanently inhibited by an outside show of force.

So, as the work of Phase III began – the consolidation of Phase II gains, as well as a broadening and consolidation of existing Humanitarian Relief Sectors – minds began to focus on the difficult process that lay in Phase IV, that of identifying the point at which UNITAF would allow itself to be superseded by the United Nations, UNOSOM II effectively, with many salient voices beginning to express concern that with the removal of the United States as the mailed fist of the operation, anarchic conditions would very quickly return.

CHAPTER THREE: UNOSOM II

War is merely the continuation of policy by other means
– Carl von Clausewitz

The New Year of 1992/3 saw two high-profile visitors to the Somali theatre. US president, George Bush, arrived to visit troops, and generally to celebrate the success of this first purely humanitarian operation to be undertaken under the patronage of the United States as the sole remaining superpower. At the same time, the secretary-general of the United Nations, Boutros Boutros-Ghali, arrived in the Somali capital to assess the situation on the ground and, perhaps, to serve as a reminder that his too was a voice to consider in the upcoming political contest that would define the end of UNITAF's role in the Somali crisis.

President Bush, generally warmly received in Somalia, was anxious to highlight the accomplishment of Operation Restore Hope as a symbol of the success of his one-term administration, recently overturned by the victory of Arkansas governor, Bill Clinton. Addressing troops in Baidoa, Bush stressed his commitment to bringing US troops home as soon as possible and handing the operation over to the United Nations. Boutros-Ghali, representing the United Nations, arrived in country at more or less the same time. His was a disastrous three-hour flying visit that prompted a noisy and potentially violent demonstration, which prevented him from holding meetings planned with various UN, American and relief officials. Later, at a hastily convened press conference at the airport, Boutros-Ghali appeared shaken and angry. He dismissed the demonstration as unrepresentative, which it probably was, despite it leaving him professionally humiliated and, privately, even more deeply antipathetic towards Aidid than at any time prior.

For his part, Aidid, who felt satisfied that he had made his point, meekly attended the UN-organized Conference on National Reconciliation in Somalia that was held soon afterwards in Addis Ababa and, with his fingers crossed behind his back, he joined the leaders of 15 separate militant Somali organizations in signing a reconciliation and disarmament agreement, the Addis Ababa Agreement (1993). To him, entreaties from both the UN representative, Ismat Kittani, and Robert Oakley to accept and respect the fact that ultimately overall responsibility for relief operations in Somalia would return to the UN, was

UN Moroccan jeeps, armed with anti-tank weapons, and personnel prepare to depart their base camp for another checkpoint, in support of UNOSOM II.

US president, George Bush

US president, Bill Clinton

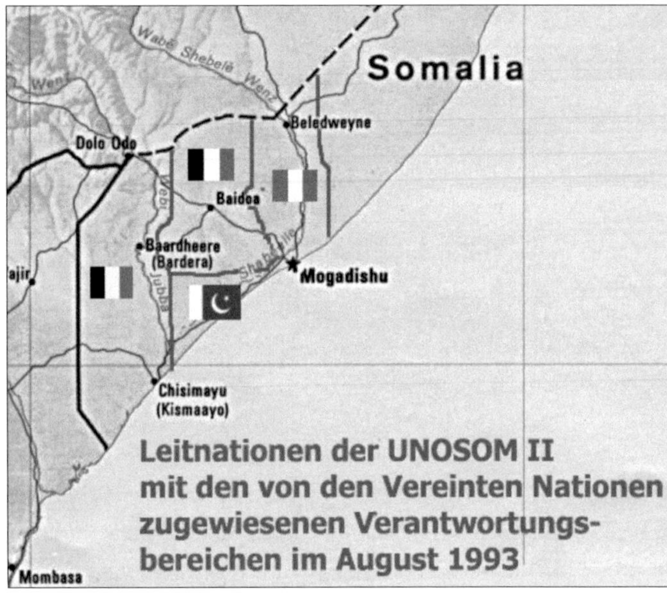

Map of Somalia, with responsible areas of the UNOSOM II mission, August 1993.

Lieutenant-General Anthony Zinni, Combined Task Force commander, US Marine Corps, at Moi International Airport. Zinni is being briefed on the progress of US forces bringing in personnel, material and equipment to support the operation which is the withdrawal of United Nations peacekeepers from Mogadishu

little more than notice being served that the military restrictions currently placed on him and his rivals were not open-ended, and notwithstanding any undertakings committed to paper, the civil war in Somalia was by no means over.

The question, simply, became one of what would represent conditions deemed broadly suitable for the transition of responsibility for general security within Somalia by UNOSOM from UNITAF. The point needs to be made that the crisis in Somalia does not represent, in any regard, the finest hour of the United Nations, and arguably Boutros-Ghali was a disastrous secretary-general in regard to Somalia. In general, however, it must, in fairness, be added that he presided over a transitional period for the United Nations that would have challenged men far more gifted than him. A few days earlier he been jeered in Sarajevo as he appealed to the government not to open a military offensive to break the siege of that city. Bearing in mind his national origins, however, and the history of the United Nations in Somalia (prompt abandonment in the aftermath of Siad Barre's ouster), Boutros-Ghali's most damaging diplomatic malfunction was in failing to recognize that it was arguably he who represented the greatest obstacle to UN success in the region.

What was inescapable, however, was the fact that trouble would once again begin to brew the moment that US military muscle was removed from the theatre. If two parties wish to fight, then a fight will take place. It can hardly be regarded as hysteria, therefore, that Boutros-Ghali insisted, as an absolute minimum, that full disarmament precede an American withdrawal but, at the same time, it can hardly be regarded as intransigent that the Americans broadly refused to countenance this.

Tensions between the US government and the UN were already noticeable during late 1992 as momentum towards some sort of substantive US response was beginning to build. This was characterized by generally unfriendly discussions that were held between secretary of state, Lawrence Eagleburger, and Boutros-Ghali during late November, and further aggravated by an exchange of letters that followed between the White House and Boutros-Ghali in December.

In reply to a letter from Boutros-Ghali, President Bush has been quoted as saying: 'I want to emphasize that the mission of the coalition is limited and specific: to create security conditions which will permit the feeding of the starving Somali people and allow the transfer of these security functions to the UN peacekeeping force.'

In essence, the two bickered over the extent of the UNITAF mandate, with the United States, with most coalition partners in agreement, arguing for strict limitations, and Boutros-Ghali insisting on a much wider scope of operations, broader geographic parameters and longer duration. Implicit in this was the belief

Truckloads of Somalis travelling out of Baidoa.

US secretary of state, Lawrence Eagleburger

that only the United States possessed the capacity to carry out a sufficiently comprehensive disarmament in Somalia for the situation on the ground to even approach a level of stabilization acceptable for a UN takeover.

The issue pivoted on disarmament, and the gulf between what the United Nations regarded as essential and what the United States recognized as possible. The issue was so fraught with difficulty, and was so rich with interpretation (gun control imposed on any nation by the United States struck many in the satirical press as ironic), that the question was deliberately excluded from the terms of the mission, leaving the commander on the ground to determine, according to conditions, what level of weapons control he felt was practical. Lieutenant-General Johnston, in turn, allowed his subordinate commanders on a sectoral level a similarly wide power of discretion over the matter. Chief of Operations, Anthony Zinni, coined the pragmatic term 'deconfliction', which serves very well to define the position.

In general, the cantonment of heavy weapons and the removal of 'technicals' from the streets were considered acceptable. The seizure of weapons caches was undertaken where possible, individual weapons confiscated where necessary and, for the rest, an understanding was reached between UNITAF and the warlords that overt gunplay, or aggression of any sort, would result in a prompt slap-down, which, in rare instances, was precisely what happened. In regard to the wholesale removal of weapons from the theatre, it was simply not practical. Too many weapons were in circulation and too much importance was placed on the individual right to bear arms – besides which, insecurity countrywide was such, that disarming one clan would simply ensure its destruction at the hands of another. Another key point was that the veneer of cordiality under which the entire operation was proceeding would be comprehensively shattered at the moment that a broad programme of disarmament was rolled out. As a consequence US military planners shied away from the whole idea, and quite reasonably so.

The protracted squabble that ensued succeeded only in delaying planning. It seems that Boutros-Ghali genuinely believed that if enough pressure could be maintained on the US for long enough it would acquiesce, which continued until April 1993, meaning, in practical terms, that the procedure-driven structure of the United Nations found itself confronting a transition in Somalia without a formal plan to cover disarmament, demobilization and the reintegration of Somali militias into civilian life. When UNOSOM II came into being in early March 1993, no detailed plan was in place. It was here that the first glimmer of opportunity presented itself to the warlords.

Both Ismat Kittani and chief United Nations military observer, Lieutenant-General Imtiaz Shaheen, were absent from their posts at this crucial moment, on grounds of health, so something of a vacuum of leadership existed at UNOSOM headquarters in Somalia but, in actual fact, even had either man been present, authorization to proceed with planning for the UNOSOM takeover lay with neither, so paralysis would have been the net result anyway. Blame lay with the secretary-general and his inability to concede diplomatic defeat over the UNITAF mandate and, to some extent, also with the structure and mindset of the United Nations itself. Manifestly, the United Nations was in no position to assume the responsibility being prepared for it, and as this gloomy state of affairs was pondered, the organization did nothing to prepare itself. Quite obviously the warlords, and Aidid most particularly, would quickly detect a scent of blood in the water, and would soon be circling around the United Nations in observance of its vulnerability.

It was not until February 1993 that a head of operations was named by the United Nations secretary-general – Lieutenant-General Cevik Bir, a widely respected Turkish officer – to whom

French vehicles lined up at the port. The vehicles are to be loaded on the Russian charter ship, *Pobho*, for transport back to France.

A German soldier fills a water tank at a school in Belet Uen. The water is brought from a water-purification plant tbuilt by the Germans, in support of United Nations Operation Somalia (UNOSOM) II.

the United States immediately paired army major-general, Tom Montgomery, as deputy and commander of US forces in Somalia. Neither assumed command on the ground until March, and even then without a command staff. The identification of multinational participants was also slow to get off the ground. Italy and France indicated their willingness to contribute troops, but the Australians and the Canadians made it known that all their troops would be removed from Somalia by May and June respectively. Efforts to increase the number of Pakistani troops in the theatre hinged on a waiver of legislation barring US military cooperation with Pakistan. India proved extremely coy to share a bed with Pakistan, and was extremely slow in delivering on a commitment to provide a brigade of 4,500 troops. In April, 3,500 Pakistani troops were deployed into the theatre, bringing their numbers up to 4,000, but they arrived ill-equipped. At this point, the United Nations had troop commitments to both the former Yugoslavia and Cambodia, as well as ongoing operations in Mozambique, Angola and elsewhere, and was technically and financially overstretched.

This immediately begged the question, how would the high standards of logistical support so far provided to UNITAF by the US be continued once the United Nations assumed responsibility for funding and after the US withdrawal. By then, Bill Clinton was in office, and despite a generally clear-spoken commitment for substantial US support for UNOSOM, details were vague. In fact, the United States would contribute a robust 1,300-man quick-reaction force to provide an aggressive emergency response capability in support of a generally lacklustre international capability. In addition the Marine Expeditionary Unit operating in the Indian Ocean–Persian Gulf region would be made available, along with all of the US in-place logistical equipment currently in use by UNITAF. The total US manpower commitment, including the deputy commander, Major-General Tom Montgomery, would be 4,000 men.

In the hope of securing a more committed alliance with the US, the UN invited Washington to suggest a replacement for Ismat Kittani, who was due to retire after several months of somewhat indifferent service as the UN Special Representative for Somalia. The name put forward was US navy Admiral Jonathan Howe, a suggestion accepted with alacrity by Boutros-Ghali. Howe, who had served as deputy national security adviser to President Bush on both Operation Restore Hope and Somalia, would partner Lieutenant-General Cevik Bir in the civilian/diplomatic role.

Although Howe had been hand-selected for this appointment by US National Security Adviser Anthony Lake, the official language emerging from the White House on the matter was carefully configured to imply that this was a UN, not a US appointment, and, as if to reinforce the point, Oakley stepped down immediately prior to Howe assuming his responsibilities, leaving no doubt that it was the United Nations that carried

Somali students in a classroom set up by UNOSOM mission staff.

ultimate responsibility to see the process through or, at the very least, would be *seen* to have that responsibility.

On 26 March, the United Nations Security Council adopted Resolution 814, calling for the replacement of UNITAF forces with a UN peacekeeping force that, for the first time in the history of the UN, was established under Chapter VII of the UN Charter. This effectively empowered the United Nations to 'determine the existence of any threat to the peace, breach of the peace, or act of aggression' and to take military and non-military action to 'restore international peace and security'. With typical indifference to practical reality, two key objectives were established. These were: to provide for the consolidation, expansion and maintenance of a secure environment throughout Somalia, and the rehabilitation of the political institutions and economy of Somalia.

Interestingly, however, Admiral Howe was able to switch sides quite neatly as soon as he assumed his UN responsibilities. Almost from the moment that he was confirmed as a UN appointee, he too began to recognize, and comment upon, the anomalies of the stage where the last act of the Somali drama was scheduled to play out. Soon after his arrival in Somalia, he approached Johnston and Zinni, urging both to consider not only delaying the dismantling of UNITAF, but also a wider deployment. Failing in this, Howe, eagerly supported by Boutros-Ghali, then sought to lobby through his high-level US military and civil contacts for enlarging and extending UNITAF's mandate. He found in his path, however, the immovable obstacle of CENTCOM commander, General Joseph Hoar, who insisted that UNITAF had fulfilled its mandate and that any further action would imply a new mission for which fresh presidential approval for the assignment of resources would be required.

The official date of the handover of responsibility from UNITAF to UNOSOM was scheduled for 4 May 1993. By the time UN officials in Mogadishu received notification of this, the US Marines had already largely left the country.

A sense of gloom descended over the local UN administration as the news of this sank in, and almost tangibly the dynamic military/civil partnership of Johnston/Oakley devolved into a bureaucratic and procedural regime, replete with barriers and repetitions, and a general distancing from one another of the three principal branches of UNOSOM II: political, humanitarian and military.

An overall sense that UNOSOM was ill equipped to take on the task could not be shaken, coupled with the obvious fact that the Somalis recognized that the operation was weak and vulnerable to challenge. Admiral Howe was heard to comment rather morbidly: 'The early May change of command marked the transformation of the force from one dominated by a superpower with more than 20,000 troops of its own on the ground to one led by a weak organization of many small contingents, the largest being 4,000 Pakistanis still waiting for a portion of their equipment.'

If nothing else, the abrupt removal from the streets of Mogadishu of the not-to-be-messed-with US Marine Corps had a profound

A UN Saudi Arabian high-mobility multi-purpose wheeled vehicle (HMMWV), with a QCB machine gun mounted on top, departs for the port of Mogadishu.

effect on the Somalis, in particular those loyal to Aidid, that could not be dispelled by the continued presence in the capital of ARFOR in the form of the 10th Mountain Division, now known as the Quick Reaction Force (QRF). Tangible signs of a drawing in of the UNOSOM peacekeeping role in Mogadishu were also not lost on the Somalis. Day and night patrols were sharply reduced, and, of course, the image presented of nervous Pakistani units on the streets of the capital could hardly compensate for the removal of the aggressive and well-supported Marine patrols. More or less under the noses of UNOSOM, Aidid immediately began to reinsert his heavy weaponry into Mogadishu, while, at the same time, broadcasts from his private radio station took on a noticeably more aggressive tone.

A point worth making is that under UNITAF, a programme of nation-building had been underway for some time. This was undertaken as an effort to empower village councils and traditional leaders as an alternative to the Kalashnikov diplomacy of Aidid and other warlords. This, naturally, tended to marginalize the warlords, and prune their local influence, which affected Aidid perhaps more than any other, and so it was he who was most anxious to start pushing back the moment that the military muscle of UNITAF was withdrawn. His radio station was a key weapon in his arsenal, the emanations from which were a fairly accurate gauge of his mood and temper. And, of course, it surprised few that upon the handover from UNITAF to UNOSOM, Aidid almost immediately began to devolve from the previously compliant, if somewhat prickly, personality of yore into the aggressive, militant and paranoid demagogue of popular mythology. Both the United Nations and the United States quickly began to recognize Aidid himself as the main obstacle to the successful implementation of Resolution 814, particularly since his opponent, Ali Mahdi, appeared to bask in the sunlight of United Nations' approval, and could anticipate that within an imposed democratic solution that it would be he who would likely triumph. The raising of tensions between UNOSOM and Aidid, therefore, did absolutely nothing to deflect the inevitability of a contest of arms, and when, on 4 June 1993, Aidid was informed by UNOSOM that the SNA weapons inventory would be inspected the following day, the stage for a confrontation was set.

This event would prove to be the turning point in the entire multi-national engagement in Somalia. The UNOSOM notification had been preceded by widespread rumours, propagated in no small part by Aidid's own propaganda machine, that these weapons inspections were nothing more than a ruse to target Radio Mogadishu, Aidid's radio station, which happened to be co-located at one of the five Authorizd Weapons Storage Sites (AWSSs) earmarked for inspection. It must be remembered that, by that point, Somali civilian spies had comprehensively penetrated the UN structure, meaning that Aidid would have been fully apprised on UNOSOM plans and objectives as they were being tabled. He was naturally suspicious of the stated objectives of the weapons inspections, and reacted accordingly. It is worth pointing out here that, although silencing Aidid's main propaganda voice was certainly a general objective of UNOSOM, it was not specifically part of the 5 June operation.

Trouble began at the radio station compound almost as soon as troops arrived. A somewhat choreographed crowd of angry Somalis began to appear on the scene as the inspection got underway, presaging a tactic that would solidify in the weeks and months to come. An area would be deliberately flooded by women and children, all displaying an overtly confrontational and aggressive attitude, while in the midst of the throng militants would penetrate and attack, using the crowd as a human shield. This was in obvious recognition of the fact that the normal standards of military discipline, and the carefully composed rules of engagement defined for the operation, would not allow troops to fire on ostensibly unarmed civilians.

Despite the presence of an angry mob, the weapons inspection mission went ahead according to plan. However, shortly thereafter, as it was en route back towards the main city stadium where the Pakistani contingent was based, a Pakistani escort unit ran into a carefully orchestrated ambush. An intense firefight then ensued, with the trapped convoy receiving enormous volumes of small-arms, automatic and rocket-propelled-grenade fire. Calls for reinforcements went out, which had been anticipated by the Somalis, who then ambushed the relief vehicles, resulting in a second sustained action. In the subsequent chaos, Italian helicopters inadvertently fired on their own side, while all over the battle periphery makeshift obstacles and roadblocks were being positioned to hinder both escape and the approach of relieving

The High Mobility Multipurpose Wheeled Vehicle (HMMWV, colloquially the 'Humvee') is a family of light, four-wheel drive, military trucks and utility vehicles. Manufactured by AM General, it supplanted numerous earlier vehicles, including different versions of the M151 jeep and other light trucks. Designed for the transport of personnel and light cargo on the front lines, its basic version, the M998 shown here, offered no ballistic armour nor protection against atomic, biological or chemical threats. However, its chassis proved highly survivable, and even vehicles heavily damaged by small arms fire during urban combat in Mogadishu carried the majority of their crews to safety. (Artwork by David Bocquelet)

As of 2022, there are about 20 different variants of the HMMWV in service with the US armed forces. The one most widely deployed in Somalia – and the one that saw most action during Operation Gothic Serpent – was the M1025 Armament Carrier (without winch). This example, armed with the Mk.19 40mm grenade launcher, was in service with the US Army's Military Police at Mogadishu International Airport in October 1992. (Artwork by David Bocquelet)

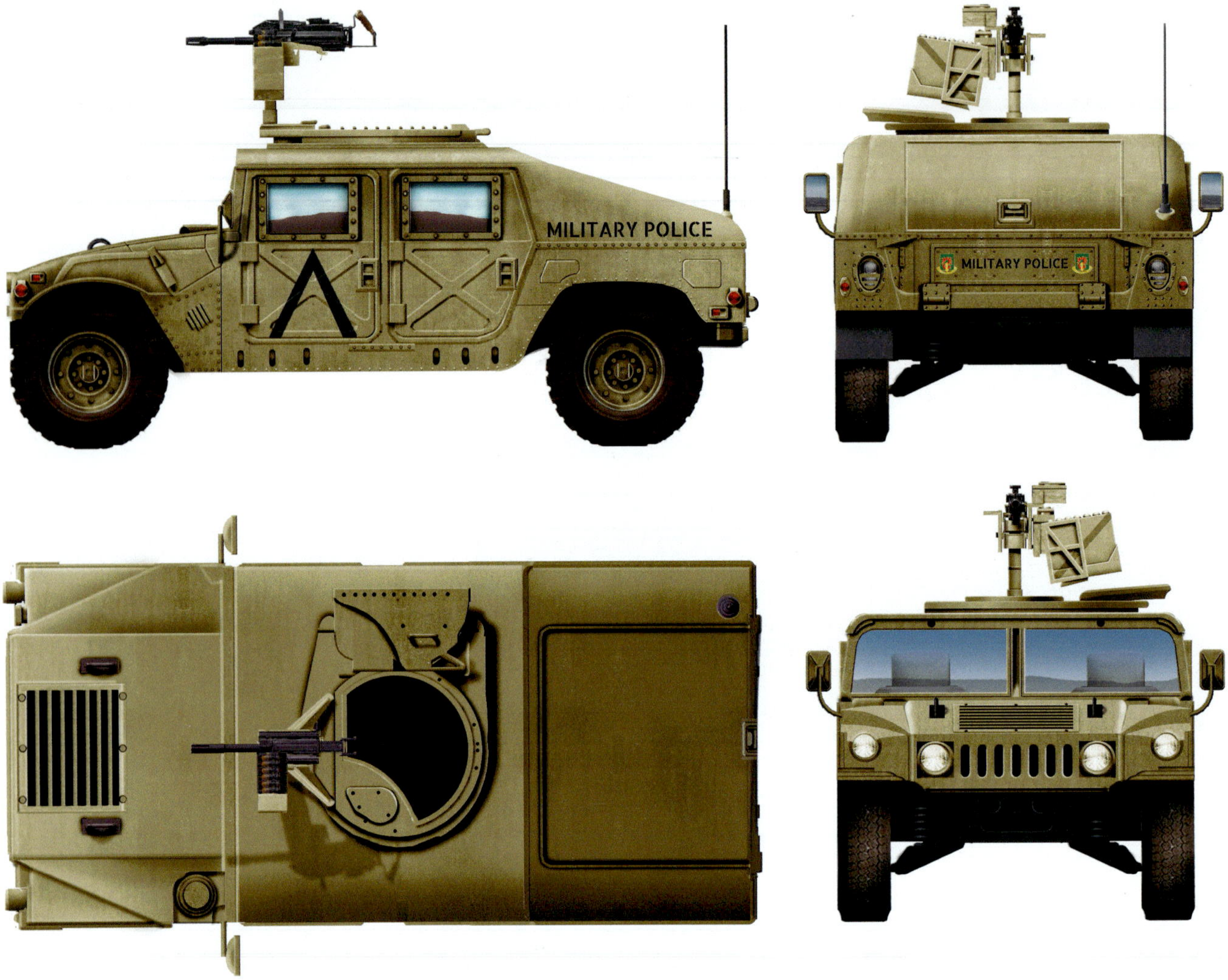

A four-sided projection of another M1025 Armament Carrier of the US Military Police, also armed with the Mk.19 grenade launcher, seen in Mogadishu in 1992–1993. Notable are the unit insignia applied on the rear door, and the chevron/inverted V in black, that has been applied as a visual identification aid during the earlier Operation Desert Storm. The majority – though not all – of the US Army and US Marines' vehicles deployed in Somalia (and the Humvees of the Royal Saudi Ground Forces' contingent of UNOSOM) still wore the desert tan (FS33446) CARC colour applied overall. (Artwork by David Bocquelet)

This M240-armed M1025 was assigned to C Company of the 1st Battalion, 87th Infantry Regiment – the first US Army unit deployed to Somalia in support of Operation Restore Hope. The battalion was attached to 2-87 Infantry to form TF.2-87, which became involved in numerous missions, including assaults on militia strongholds in Beledweyne, multiple cordon and search operations, and ran into several ambushes. While attached to the 2-14 Infantry Regiment, C Company 1-87 became involved in the Battle of Mogadishu. (Artwork by David Bocquelet)

The US Marines in Somalia relied heavily on their Light Armoured Vehicles – the LAV-25 – an eight-wheeled amphibious armoured reconnaissance vehicle. Part of a family of vehicles built by General Dynamics Land Systems that included command, recovery, TOW and mortar vehicles, the main variant shown here was armed with the M242 Bushmaster 25mm chain gun, mounted (with 210 rounds of ammunition) in a turret with 360° traverse. Installed co-axially was a 7.62mm M240 machine gun: a second – pintle-mounted – M240 was part of the standard equipment but was frequently removed, as shown here. Note the extensive stowage of personal kit on the exterior of the vehicle, including items in the 'chocolate chip' desert camouflage pattern. (Artwork by David Bocquelet)

After years of civil war, very few of the 'regular' military vehicles of the former Somali Army were still in operational condition and operated by local militias by 1992-1993: the mass of those still around was destroyed by UN troops. However, Aideed's militia did have several survivors from around 270 Italian-made Fiat/Oto Melara Type 6614 and 6616 armoured personnel carriers, donated by Rome in the 1980s. Made of steel, the Type 6614 was usually armed with a single, pintle-mounted 7.62mm machine gun; the Type 6616 with a 20mm autocannon. The same APCs were also operated by the Italian contingent of UNOSOCM. (Artwork by David Bocquelet)

The primary 'fighting vehicle' of the mass of Somali militias were so-called 'technicals': essentially, civilian pick-up trucks or SUVs, carrying a heavy machine gun on their rear deck. This Toyota Land Cruiser GRJ79 is shown armed with a 14.5mm ZPU-1 heavy machine gun – which was one of the most common configurations. While the Somalis usually preferred vehicles painted in white (because the colour reflects the sun and thus some of the heat), examples have been seen in a very wide range of colours, including blue and red. (Artwork by David Bocquelet)

Sikorsky CH-53E Super Stallion helicopters of the US Marine Corps were the first military aircraft to become involved in Somalia. During Operation Eastern Exit, on 4 January 1991, four Super Stallions of HMH-461 from USS *Guam* (LPH-9) were used to deploy 60 Marines and Navy SEALs to evacuate US diplomatic personnel from the embassy in Mogadishu. Over the following three years, additional CH-53Es and MH-53Es saw periodic deployments to Somalia within the framework of operations Provide Relief and Provide Hope. All wore a standardised camouflage pattern in two greys (FS36375 overall, and FS35237 on top surfaces), service titles, and two-digit modex numbers on the nose and the fuselage sides. (Artwork by Luca Canossa)

A total of ten C-130s and 400 airmen of the US Air Force were deployed to Mombasa, in Kenya, in support of Operation Provide Relief from August 1992. They airlifted aid to Somalia's remote areas and thus reduced reliance on truck convoys, which were vulnerable to ambushes. When this proved inadequate, Operation Restore Hope was launched in December 1992, and the number of C-130s further increased – in part through the addition of examples operated by the Australian, Belgian, Canadian, and French air forces. Amongst those of the US Air Force rotated through the operation in 1993 were C-130Hs of the 773rd Air Squadron, 463rd Air Wing, Kentucky Air National Guard, one of which is illustrated here. (Artwork by Tom Cooper)

AC-130H Spectre gunships of the 16th SOS were repeatedly deployed over Somalia, primarily from Mombasa in Kenya. On 14 March 1993, while en route from Kenya to Somalia, this AC-130H (FY-serial 69-6576, nick-named the 'Predator') suffered a detonation of its 105mm gun. Heavy damage followed by a spreading fire forced the crew to ditch into the Indian Ocean near Milindi in Kenya: three crewmembers bailed out, while the pilot, co-pilot and flight engineer survived the ditching. As far as is known, the Predator still wore the Europe 1 camouflage pattern at the time of its demise, consisting of grey (FS36118), green (FS34092) and green (FS34102), which was badly worn out by local elements. (Artwork by Tom Cooper)

The 160th Special Operations Aviation Regiment (Airborne) of the US Army was established after the failed hostage rescue attempt in Iran in 1980. For operations in Somalia it deployed a mix of MD.530E-based AH-6J and MH-6J Little Birds, of which the former were usually armed with two M134 miniguns and two M260 7-shot Hydra 70 2.75" pods. The MH-6s, one of which is shown here, were unarmed but equipped to carry up to six passengers on external benches. While only one AH-6J – FY-serial 90-25362/Barber 52 – played an active role in Operation Gothic Serpent, the entire Star Flight of four MH-6Js became involved: shown here is the example with serial number 981-23635/Star Flight 44. (Artwork by Pablo Albornoz)

This MH-60L (91-26324, nick-named *Thunderstruck*) of the 160th SOAR had the call-sign 'Super 61' during Operation Gothic Serpent in Mogadishu on 3–4 October 1994, and was one of two shot down (the other was Super 64/89-26188/*Venom*). All were painted in matt black overall (bleached to anthracite by elements), and all (except for Super 63/90-26257/*Grim Reaper*) had their call-signs painted in black on the front window of the cargo doors. Pilot doors were usually removed; some retained their FLIR and radar domes, but others had these, angled missile plume detectors and IFR-probes removed. No ESSS wings were attached, but all had tail-mounted APR-39 radar detectors. (Artwork by Pablo Albornoz)

While two MH-60Ls were shot down during Operation Gothic Serpent, three others suffered heavy damage but were able to land under power. These were Super 62/83-23882/*Black Widow*, Super 66/85-24395/*Predator*, and the MH-60L shown here, Super 68/90-26288/*Razors Edge*. The Super 62 took an RPG-7 hit into the position of the mini-gunner (who lost a leg, but survived), yet was still recovered, repaired and subsequently served with the Multinational Force & Observers mission in Sinai, Egypt. Super 68/*Razors Edge* continued serving with the 160th SOAR for years longer and was significantly modified before ending its days at the Army Aviation Museum at Fort Rucker in Alabama. (Artwork by Pablo Albornoz)

US Army troops on the streets of Mogadishu, shortly after the start of Operation Restore Hope, in 1992. (US DoD)

A Marine of the 15th Marine Expeditionary Unit manning a M249 squad automatic weapon (SAW) atop an AAVP-7A1 amphibious assault vehicle, while en route to Mogadishu International, during Operation Restore Hope. (US DoD)

A LAV-25 of the USMC's 3rd Light Armoured Infantry Battalion (left) and a Fiat/Oto Melara 6616 armoured personnel carrier (the variant with a 20mm autocannon turret) of the Italian Army (right), seen guarding an intersection on the 'Green Line' in Mogadishu. (US DoD)

A column of Condor APCs of the Malaysian contingent of UNOSOM. These were used to help extract US troops from the dense urban centre of Mogadishu: one Malaysian soldier was killed and seven injured in this action. (Photo by CT Snow)

A Bell UH-1N of the US Marine Corps lifting off from the ramp of Moi International, outside Mombasa in Kenya. The helicopter was one of an entire fleet used to ferry personnel and equipment to and from naval vessels off the coast of Africa during the withdrawal of United Nations peacekeeping forces (UNOSOM II) from Somalia in 1994. (US DoD)

Somalia
and neighbouring countries
1992-1994
Asmara
ERITREA
Sana'a
YEMEN
Aden
DJIBOUTI
Djibouti
Dire Dawa
Hargeisa
Harar
Adis Ababa
ETHIOPIA
Bandarbeyla
Garowe
Galkayo
SOMALIA
Beledweyne
Baidoa
Jowhar
Bardere
Mogadishu
Merca
KENYA
Kismayo
Nairobi
Malindi
Mombasa
TANZANIA
Dar es-Salaam
0 km
200
400
600
800

forces. Scattered firefights took place as the fighting continued into the afternoon.

In the meanwhile, a second significant action was taking place as angry Somalis mobbed a Pakistani platoon guarding a food distribution site, shielding militiamen as they crept forward and opened fire. By then, the Pakistani soldiers had already allowed the crowd to advance close enough to obstruct their weapons. Pinned down, the Pakistanis were eventually relieved by the Quick Reaction Forces and Italian armoured units, but not before 24 of their number had been killed and scores of others wounded, with yet others taken captive. Three American soldiers and an Italian were also wounded.

This episode effectively marked the end of the *Pax Americana* that had held the peace in Somalia since the deployment of UNITAF. An emergency debate was held in the Security Council the following day, which resulted in the unanimous adoption of Security Council Resolution 837.* Here, the United Nations appeared to accept, without any formal inquiry, the culpability of the United Somali Congress–Somali National Alliance for the attacks that took place on 5 June 1993. In a surprising display of anger and unanimity, all necessary measures were authorized to bring to account those responsible, with a specific decision made to effect the arrest of Mohamed Farah Aidid. Implied in this resolution, although not specifically stated, was a go-ahead for the enhanced military steps that were subsequently taken against Aidid and his senior associates. It was a *de facto* declaration of war, at which point military operations gradually began to succeed humanitarian operations as the main thrust of UNOSOM II.

The United Nations was effectively now fighting a counter-insurgency campaign.

* The resolution was drawn up in haste by US UN ambassador, Madeleine K. Albright, in consultation with Anthony Lake and Ambassador Howe. General Colin Powell was not consulted.

CHAPTER FOUR: TASK FORCE RANGER

During a discussion shortly after my arrival in country with the outgoing QRF commander, I asked what he thought was the worst case scenario we might have to respond to. Without hesitation, he said it would be an aircraft forced down in the Black Sea
[an extremely hostile neighbourhood of Mogadishu]
– Colonel Lawrence E Casper,
QRF Commander

A highly instructive observation was made by air force combat controller, Dan Schilling, in a brief memoir of the iconic battle that occurred in the streets of Mogadishu over 3/4 October 1993. Schilling had just arrived in Mogadishu as part of Task Force Ranger, and was observing a firefight underway between two rival Somali factions:

> After requesting an MH-60 [Sikorsky UH-60 Black Hawk] from the JOC, I gave the aircraft that showed up a brief description of the situation down the road and asked him to do a flyby. He made a pass from our location over the Somalis and so was flying away from us. We were looking down the road at the gunfire being exchanged between the locals and then we watched in amazement as both sides stopped shooting at each other and began engaging the helicopter.[9]

The irony of how things had evolved in Somalia since the iconic Marine landing of December 1992, could hardly be better illustrated than this. In a few short months, the high-minded humanitarianism that had inspired the United States and others to lend considerable weight to the alleviation of grotesque human suffering, created largely by the Somalis themselves, had gradually devolved into a situation where those trying to help were forced to fight, and to pay in blood, for the privilege of doing so. If this appeared to defy western logic, it certainly seemed to be completely rational to the Somalis. It had not only been militias that had been involved in the killing of the Pakistanis, but large numbers of civilians too, those very civilians receiving food and other aid, and those who had cheered and clapped as armed convoys rolled into the many towns and relief centres identified in Operation Restore Hope, and who had largely been the ones who had benefited from the peace imposed by the various coalition forces in order that they might be fed.

In the aftermath of 5 June, numerous incidents of violence were registered that resulted in scores of UNOSOM casualties, and hundreds more among the Somalis. On 17 June, Moroccan peacekeepers sustained heavy casualties during an attack on Aidid's enclave in southern Mogadishu, with the additional deaths reported at the hands of a mob, of several journalists who had arrived on the scene soon after the departure of the QRF.** The last straw, however, was the 8 August detonation of a remote-controlled device under a passing US Army vehicle that killed four US military policemen, followed by a landmine explosion two weeks later that injured another six. Soon afterwards, the decision was taken to form Task Force Ranger, a battle group comprising US Army Delta Force, Ranger teams, an air element

** The journalists were Hansi Krauss of Associated Press, and Dan Eldon, Hos Maina and Anthony Macharia, all of Reuters.

General Colin Powell, chairman of the Joint Chiefs of Staff

Delta Force bodyguards flank General Norman Schwarzkopf.

provided by the 160th Special Operations Aviation Regiment, four Navy SEAL operators from SEAL Team Six and members of the Air Force Pararescue/Air Force Combat Controllers, for the prosecution of what was codenamed Operation Gothic Serpent.*

With a minimum of fanfare, Task Force Ranger was flown into Mogadishu on 22 August 1993, whereupon it immediately set about achieving the capture of Mohamed Farah Aidid and any known associates. Task Force Ranger was commanded by Major-General William Garrison who was answerable directly to CENTCOM. General Montgomery, as commander of US forces in Somalia, had no direct authority over the activities of the task force at all, and was simply kept informed as a matter of protocol. Major-General William Garrison was, at that time, commander of Joint Special Operations Command (JSOC). This was a component command of the United States Special Operations Command (USSOCOM), charged with the study of special operations requirements and techniques, in order to ensure inter-operability and equipment standardization, to plan and conduct special operations exercises and training, and to develop Joint Special Operations Tactics. It was formed in 1980 in the aftermath of the failure of Operation Eagle Claw, the operation to free American hostages in Iran. Commander of Delta Force, and second-in-command to Garrison, was Colonel William Boykin.

* The key component of Task Force Ranger was the elements of 3 Ranger Battalion. There are three manoeuvre Ranger battalions in the US Army, all of which belong to the 75th Ranger Regiment, which is part of the United States Special Operations Command. Each of the Ranger battalions is commanded by a lieutenant-colonel, falling directly under the command of the Ranger regimental commander. Ranger battalions are based at three separate military installations. These are: 1st Ranger Battalion at Hunter Army Airfield, Savannah, Georgia; 2nd Ranger Battalion at Fort Lewis, Seattle-Tacoma, Washington; and 3rd Ranger Battalion at Fort Benning, Columbus, Georgia, the latter being the headquarters of the Ranger Regiment, which is commanded by a colonel. The three Ranger battalions, alongside other integral but smaller elements, make up the US Army's sole Ranger Regiment (the 75th Ranger Regiment). Each battalion maintains a high level of combat readiness at all times, with one of the three battalions designated as the Ranger Ready Force 1 (RRF1) battalion. The (RRF1) battalion will be in RRF1 status for a period of two months, twice annually. RRF1 status implies both the responsibility and the ability to deploy as a combat force anywhere in the world within 18 hours after initial alert notification, a state of readiness commonly referred to as being on a 'short string'.

The decision to insert special operations forces into Somalia to take care of Aidid as arguably the main obstacle to the success of the UNOSOM operation, was not one that was easily taken and, according to the chairman of the Joint Chiefs of Staff, General Colin Powell, it was one that he quickly came to regret. There would be other decisions that Powell would also regret, perhaps most important among them the decision to reject a request from commanders on the ground for the inclusion of Lockheed AC-130 gunships as part of the equipment earmarked for Operation Gothic Serpent.** The inclusion of this, and other heavy operation equipment, such as tanks and armoured personnel carriers, all of which were held back for fear of presenting too aggressive an image of US intentions in Somalia, might have altered the complexion of one of the toughest actions fought by American forces since the Tet Offensive of 1968, and certainly it would have saved a great many lives.

The main force element of Task Force Ranger was drawn from the 3rd Ranger Battalion, commanded at that point by Colonel Danny McKnight. McKnight published a book some years later entitled, *The Streets of Mogadishu: Leadership at its Best, Political Correctness at its Worst*, in which he fulminates quite openly on the damage done by an overly political decision-making process in the matter of defining the scope and direction of hazardous military operations, such as Operation Gothic Serpent, but obviously many others as well. In the surfeit of memoir and analysis of this operation [that of 3 October 1993] that is available today, McKnight is one of few willing to acknowledge the nakedness of the king, and admit that the operation was an utter disaster. For that, he unequivocally blames the political leadership, not unjustifiably, for the deaths of 18 US servicemen who gave their lives on that fateful day in pursuit of a strictly political objective.

Pointing the finger of blame at the political decision-making process, however, only tells part of the story. There were significant operational and tactical flaws evident as well, even at the time.

** Colin Powell: 'In Late August, I reluctantly yielded to repeated requests from the field and recommended to [Les] Aspin that we dispatch the Ranger and Delta Force [an elite commando unit]. It was a decision I would later regret.'

US paratroopers boarding a C-130.

An AC-130 Hercules gunship aircraft

attacks were frequent, but usually inaccurate and seldom effective. The press had, however, been alerted to the arrival of Task Force Ranger, which meant, of course, that the fact was widely appreciated in Somalia too.

Garrison opted to take the matter personally and return the compliment hard and fast. Four days later, in the early hours of the morning, a dozen helicopters dropped a team of commandos on the roof of a building on the Via Lenin – Lig-Ligato House – rounding up and handcuffing the occupants in a matter of minutes. Prior to this, TF elements had conducted a high-profile vehicular reconnaissance of Mogadishu, with air cover provided by the task force aviation element. This aggressive and highly confident display announced fairly unequivocally that new boys were in town, and Aidid would obviously have been aware of what the job at hand was.

The operation on Lig-Ligato House was seamlessly executed, although it was later revealed that most of the captives brought in were local UN staff members, causing some amusement to conventional troops deployed in the capital, and underlining the importance, and the difficulty, of obtaining up-to-the-minute tactical intelligence in a highly fluid operational environment. In practical terms, Somalia had reverted back to a pre-electronic age, which tended to frustrate the high-tech intelligence-gathering methods that the CIA had perfected in recent years. The almost unbreakable clan bond, coupled with the awful ramifications of treachery, all tended to limit the flow of useful operational intelligence. Aidid himself was also now highly mobile and extremely well camouflaged within the rat warrens of Mogadishu.

A side incident to this operation was recorded by Colonel Danny McKnight, from the position of a vehicle convoy situated close to the Kilometre Four (K4) traffic circle, a key intersection between the major roads in the Somali capital. Wide boulevards of an imperial character had been constructed under the Italians, and, from this point, McKnight was able to observe the target building through night-vision equipment. Notice was taken of an

Overconfidence might perhaps have been one of these. The many published memoirs and biographies of the operation all tend to reveal a tangible elitism among the Rangers, and the other special force elements of the task force, over their conventional army brethren of the 10th Mountain Division. The QRF had already fought a number of actions on the streets of Mogadishu, and who had also already lost one Black Hawk helicopter to an RPG attack. Underestimating the fighting qualities and commitment of the enemy was perhaps another failure, and tactical predictability probably the most dangerous.

Task Force Ranger touched down in Mogadishu on the evening of 26 August, arriving aboard six giant C-5A Galaxy cargo jets. Their arrival was greeted by Aidid's forces with a significant mortar barrage aimed at the main airport complex. Such mortar

US Marine Corps UH-1N Huey helicopter

A sailor makes fast a UH-1N Huey of Marine Light Attack Helicopter Squadron (HMLA) 467 aboard the multi-purpose amphibious assault ship, USS *Bataan*.

danger, he succeeded in slipping the net. The episode did, however, cause Aidid to recognize that this time he was not playing with amateurs, and with a US$25,000 bounty on his head, posted by Bir and Montgomery, he knew his own people well enough to seek cover deep underground.

Recognizing this, Major-General Garrison opted to shift his focus temporarily to Aidid's six top named lieutenants – known as Tier One Personalities – upon the assumption that if you cannot take out the head, work on the body. Top of this list was Osman Ali Ato, a wealthy Somali businessman and Aidid financial strategist. During the third week of September, Ato was spotted, by chance, in a vehicle and was lifted in a timely and smooth retrieval that was almost a textbook operation of its kind. Within minutes of information being passed back to the JOC, an AH-6 Little Bird helicopter appeared overhead and two rounds were put into the engine block of Ato's car. Moments later, commandos roped down from a hovering UH-60 Black Hawk and surrounded the target, taking Osman Ato into custody without incident.

In the early hours of 25 September 1993, four days after Ato's capture, an incident occurred that was not afforded due significance at the time, but which would later be revisited as extremely significant in regards to the events that followed. On a routine night reconnaissance mission, a QRF Black Hawk helicopter – Courage 53 – was hit by an RPG rocket as it passed close to Villa Somalia, the old presidential palace. The helicopter was flying at about 100 feet over the city, displaying no lights, and at a point when the moon had dropped below the level of the horizon. The pilot struggled to maintain flight in order to reach the safety of the port area. The rocket had struck the underbelly, igniting the fuel and quickly engulfing the cargo area in flame, forcing it down in the southern quarter of Mogadishu. Three of the five crew members were killed instantly. The pilot and co-

individual standing on the hotel roof opposite the target building, who appeared to be employing an over-the-shoulder RPG. The individual was nearly obliterated by 50mm machine gun fire had McKnight not sensed the possibility that this was a member of the press with a video camera. This later turned out to be the case.

The raid on the Lig-Ligato compound was the first of seven operations undertaken by Task Force Ranger in Mogadishu during its tour. The pattern of operations was very similar from one operation to the next, with each extremely smoothly executed. The operation that immediately followed the Lig-Ligato assault very nearly succeeded in netting Aidid.

Intelligence, lean at best, had, on this occasion, indicated accurately that the warlord was present, but, perhaps sensing

A C-5 Galaxy

pilot survived and succeeded in reaching friendly lines.

In the meanwhile, the capture of Osman Ato, although satisfying, was perhaps counter-productive, since it rattled Aidid and forced him deeper underground. Persistence paid off, however, and on the morning of 3 October, a call came in from a buried 'asset' in Mogadishu indicating that a cadre of top Aidid lieutenants, including two from the Tier One list – Omar Salad Elmi and Mohamed Hassan Awale – were scheduled to meet that afternoon inside a compound located on Hawlwadig Road close to the Olympic Hotel. This was also in the same general locale as the Bakaara market, the heart of what was known as the Black Sea, deep in the SNA quarter of Mogadishu. It was also suggested that Aidid himself might attend.

The initial intelligence was received at about noon, which was the point at which indications began to circulate among the men of Task Force Ranger that an operation was afoot. To begin with, activity was focused in the operations centre. Word was radioed back to the intelligence asset to position a driver on the street outside the target building in order that an Orion spy plane in circulation overhead, beaming real-time video imagery onto screens in the operations centre, and surveillance Black Hawks, also in relatively constant attendance over Mogadishu, could pinpoint the exact location.

As Task Force Ranger busied itself for action, communications continued with the buried asset who appeared to be displaying some reluctance to approach the actual target building, and required some talking through his prevarication. At 15h00, a provisional go was given for the launch of the operation, although the signal for launch – codeword Irene – would not be given without 100 per cent confirmation that the targets were *in situ*. Such confirmation was received at the Task Force operations centre at approximately 15h30.

The Battle of Mogadishu occurred during the late afternoon, consuming the remainder of that day and the subsequent hours of darkness between 3 and 4 October 1993. As such, it did not play out over many hours, but a great deal took place in the evolution of the battle during that time period, with certain parallel sequences initiating a cascading cause and effect, all of which culminated in what was inescapably an operational fiasco.

The risks of the operation were not insignificant. Entering the heart of the Black Sea – the epicentre of SNA-controlled turf – in broad daylight, after having exposed the Somalis militias to several general repetitions of the same tactics, was certainly very risky. The Quick Reaction Force Black Hawk that had been shot down on 25 September was deemed to have been brought down by a lucky RPG hit.

There was, however, some suggestion made that perhaps the Somalis were adapting their response to the US commando strategy by flooding the field with RPGs and attempting to draw helicopters into an ambush. It was widely expected that if significant casualties could be wrought on US troops, a withdrawal would quickly follow.

Launching a mid-afternoon assault would also have put troops in harm's way at the peak of the general khat effect, at which point Somali militiamen, numbers of whom had been steadily migrating to the city in support of operations against the coalition, could be expected to be as energetic and ready to brawl as any time during the day.

Planning for the operation of 3 October followed more or less the same pattern as previous operations. Four light AH-6Js would each carry four snipers, two seated on either side of the helicopter, somewhat exposed to the elements, yet also in an extremely versatile operating position. Each of the Little Birds was armed with rocket pods mounted beneath. Another four AH-6Js, armed with 7.62mm Miniguns* and 2.75-inch rockets, would cover and protect the front and rear of the target building. Delta C Squadron operatives would fast-rope onto the roof of the target building from two MH-6 Little Birds, from where they would penetrate the building and conduct a sweep and snatch.

A hard-hitting force of eight UH-60 Black Hawk helicopters would follow, two of which would be carrying Delta assaulters and their ground command, and four would each be loaded with

* The M134 Minigun is a 7.62mm, six-barrelled machine gun with an extremely high rate of fire - some 2,000 to 6,000 rounds per minute – and which employs a Gatling-style system of rotating barrels powered by an electric motor.

a Ranger 'chalk' – parlance for a specific aircraft load – to four points located at each corner of the target building. The Rangers would be inserted by fast-rope in order to immediately establish a security cordon. At the same time, a vehicle convoy would arrive alongside the target building, into which would be loaded the captives, the Delta Force operators and the Ranger chalks, for a quick and smooth extraction. All this would be undertaken at lightning speed, and ideally wrapped up before the Somali militias were able to effectively respond. An eighth Black Hawk would have on board two mission commanders, one coordinating the pilots and one directing the men on the ground. In addition, three OH-58D Kiowa helicopters, essentially a Bell helicopter configured for observation and direct fire support, would occupy the airspace above the target to provide real-time audio and video of events on the ground directly to the Joint Operations Centre (JOC). High above this would be circling a P-3 Orion spy plane.

CHAPTER FIVE: THE BATTLE OF MOGADISHU

The Somalis were a curious bunch. For every armed person, there were fifty unarmed just standing around, often right next to the guy firing at us
– Michael Goffena, Black Hawk pilot

At 15h32, codeword Irene was issued and the mission began. The air flotilla lifted off for an estimated three-minute flight to the target area. At more or less the same time, the ground convoy moved off. The ground convoy comprised seven Kevlar Humvees, two unarmoured cargo Humvees and three five-ton trucks. The convoy was manned primarily by Ranger elements, but included Navy SEALs and a US Air Force combat controller. At 15h40, two AH-6 Apache gunships ran a last-minute flight over the target building, before four MH-6 Little Bird attack helicopters dropped 16 Delta Force soldiers close to the building for the main assault. Moments later, two Black Hawks dropped off a further 30 special operations soldiers to conduct close-in security and assist the assault team.

As this was underway, the four Ranger chalks, comprising about 16 men each, were fast-roped into position in a highly choreographed sequence, which was complicated somewhat in this environment by an almost immediate obscuring of the LZ by a mass of dust and debris blown up from the unpaved streets below.* It was not immediately apparent to those troops exiting the hovering Black Hawks, but robust enemy fire had begun immediately. Small-arms hits were being registered on the aircraft bodies and rotor blades, but it was when RPG airbursts began to be observed that the gravity of the situation abruptly became apparent. It was clear that the Somalis had been primed to respond to low-level helicopter movement with a barrage of RPG fire, and so it would only be a matter of time before a 'bird' was hit.

The first three deployments went smoothly, but Chalk Four began to take heavy fire while still in the air, and was roped in about a block too far north of the intended drop point at the northeast corner road intersection. Under the circumstances, this was not critical, but it was complicated by a Ranger, PFC Blackburn, who missed the rope and plunged 45 feet to the street below, sustaining serious neck, head and internal injuries. Overhead, pilots were already beginning to observe and report on a rapid and ongoing influx of militiamen and civilians into the area, with a resultant increase in hostile fire – small arms and RPG. It might not unreasonably be said that the Somali response to the operation almost had about it the character of a popular uprising.

In the meanwhile, the ground convoy under the command of Lieutenant-Colonel McKnight arrived in position without action or mishap. The injured Ranger was pulled out of the street and towards the waiting vehicles under a withering enfilade of enemy fire. McKnight ordered that PFC Blackburn be evacuated back to base. The small group of vehicles selected for this mission then embarked on a harrowing journey through a hostile city whose citizenry were almost universally organizing to react. Blackburn was successfully conveyed to safety, but through an ongoing and building firestorm which cost the life of another soldier, Sergeant Dominick Pilla.

Soon after the departure of the medical evacuation convoy, the 24 captured Somalis were hurried out of the target building in flex cuffs and bundled into the waiting vehicles. As this was under way, and as the security perimeter devolved into a series of static firefights, the unthinkable happened. Black Hawk Super 61, piloted by CW4 Cliff Wolcott, was hit under the main rotor by an RPG rocket, crashing soon afterwards at a location a few blocks north of the target building. Supporting aircraft immediately attempted to determine who, if any, of the crew and passengers had survived, and to lay down suppressing fire to hold back the immediate onrush of Somali militiamen and civilians.

It was at that point that the operation began to unravel. Word was immediately sent to the QRF, located at the university compound,

* The fast-rope technique in use by US forces is an adaption of a British concept first used in a combat environment during the Falklands Campaign of 1982. It was used originally in a 'fire pole' style on a smooth nylon rope, but this has since been phased out in favour of a thick, braided rope that is easier to grip. The only specialist equipment involved, besides the rope itself, is a pair of thick leather gloves to protect against rope burn. For the rest, the system relies on technique.

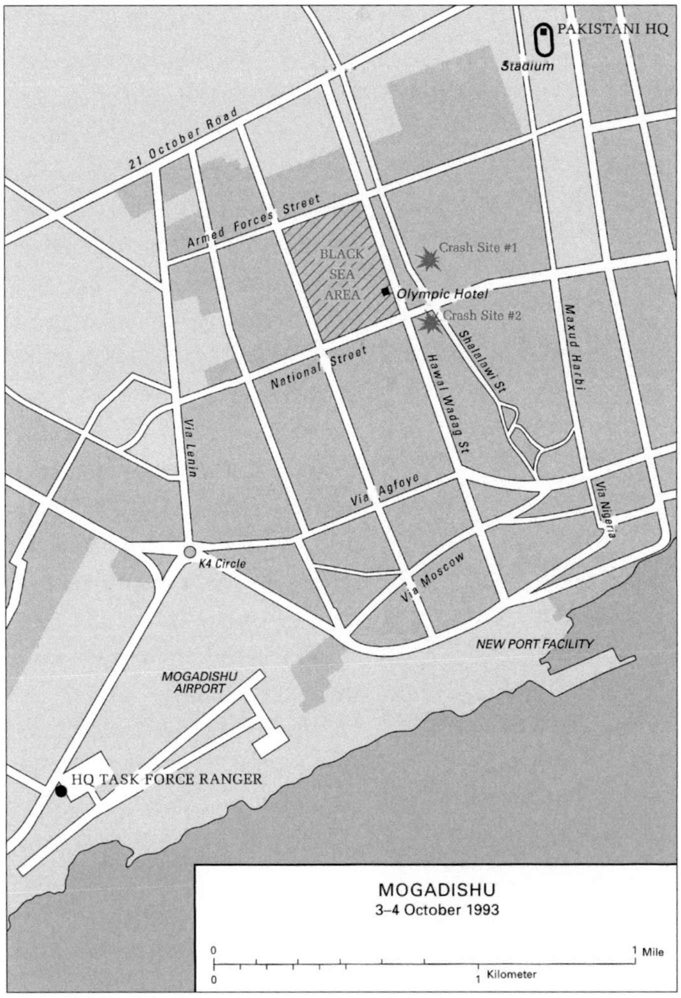

Map of Mogadishu during the 1993 Battle of Mogadishu.

The crew of Super 64 a month before the Battle of Mogadishu. From left: Winn Mahuron, Tommy Field, Bill Cleveland, Ray Frank and Mike Durant.

Bravo Company, 3rd Battalion of the 75th Ranger Regiment in Somalia, 1993.

to mobilize as soon as possible. A wholly unexpected intensity of response was amplifying moment by moment as the militias organized and were reinforced by incoming members flooding in from all parts of the city, and beyond. Makeshift barricades were being thrown up at key intersections, while palls of black smoke from the customary burning tyres were signalling far and wide that a significant engagement was underway.

The Ranger creed, no man left behind, abruptly became the creed of the operation. Ranger units heavily engaged around the target building were now forced to contemplate moving north several blocks in order to secure the crash site. The ground convoy, having sent back a detachment containing the injured Ranger to base, was further ordered to proceed to the crash site to retrieve survivors and casualties.

Thus began an almost unbelievably harrowing journey through a virtually ongoing ambush, and through streets obscured by dust, smoke and debris, alive with astronomical volumes of incoming fire and obstructed, wherever possible, by roadblocks and other obstacles. Vainly attempting to follow instructions, Lieutenant-Colonel Danny McKnight, operating under conditions that defy imagination, resolutely attempted the impossible, until, weighed down by casualties, and at risk of becoming combat-inoperable, withdrew back to base carrying numbers of casualties, and through a gauntlet of hostile action. Communications between the circling Orion spy plane, which was providing direction to the lost convoy, were conveyed first through the JOC, which resulted in a three-second delay in directional instructions being delivered to the ground. This, in the fast-moving action of the moment, caused numerous wrong turns and obstructed routes, causing the convoy to lose itself in the city while consistently engaged in heavy combat.

In the meanwhile, in an enormously courageous and technically daring action, an MH-6 Little Bird, piloted by CWO's Karl Maier and Keith Jones, dropped into the narrow confines of the urban crash scene, strung with wires and with a matter of inches of space to spare, and succeeded in rescuing two injured crew members, while at the same time attracting a surge of hostile fire from converging Somali militiamen.*

Simultaneously, an advance party of Rangers, comprising Chalk Two and part of Chalk One, arrived on the scene, having fought their way up several city blocks at the cost of several wounded and one fatality. One of the wounded would later die at the crash site. Moments later – at 16h48 – a combat search and rescue (CSAR) team arrived overhead and fast-roped in from a hovering Black Hawk, which itself took a direct hit from an RPG rocket. In one of the celebrated actions of the operation, pilot Dan Jallota held the aircraft in a hover until the CSAR team was on the ground, before

* One WIA would later die of his injuries.

Condor APCs

Staff Sergeat James Bradsher demonstrates the use of a Soviet-made RPG-7 portable rocket launcher.

limping off towards the airfield where it crash-landed.

All this had taken place within less than an hour. The Delta and Ranger deployments had begun at 15h42, and Super 61 was brought down at 14h20, 40 minutes or so from the first arrival of US troops on the scene. By 14h30, Karl Maier and Keith Jones had lifted off with two casualties, Rangers had begun to form a security perimeter and the combat search and rescue team had arrived and were attending to casualties, which were mounting steadily as the action progressed. By then, also, the ground convoy was on the move, fighting its way towards the scene, frustrated by unrelenting enemy fire and an inability to find a clear route in. In the meanwhile, a combination of forces (CSAR team, Ranger chalks and Delta soldiers, totalling approximately 90 men) held Crash Site One, with ongoing helicopter assistance, and under constant and heavy fire. One of the dead pilots was removed from the wreckage; the other, Cliff Wolcott, could not be removed without equipment.

At 16h26, six minutes after the crash, Super 64, piloted by CW4 Mike Durant, moved in to take the place of Super 62. Within a quarter of an hour, it too took a direct hit from an RPG rocket just below the tail rotor. It succeeded in staying briefly in the air, but soon came down heavily, coming to rest approximately a mile southwest of the target building.

Clearly at this point, the operation had been plunged into crisis, and it was at this point too that the denial of key assets – heavy operational armour to now attend to two points of irredeemable crisis, and the AC-130 gunships that would have provided vital suppressing fire – were most keenly felt. It is worth noting that as Lieutenant-Colonel McKnight toured the ambush alleys of Mogadishu in a confusion of delayed instructions, the AC-130s would have been able to provide real-time communications with the ground. This facility was enabled, and training had been undertaken in combination with AC-130s. Inclusion of this asset would almost certainly have saved lives and enabled the convoy to reach, not only Crash Site One, but very possibly Crash Site Two as well, which it was ordered to do shortly afterward.

Durant and his crew of three, Bill Cleveland, Ray Frank, and Tommy Field, survived the crash, although each was badly injured. To add to the general urgency, it was clear from the aircraft circling above that large numbers of armed and unarmed Somalis were converging on the scene and would overrun it within minutes. There was no immediate possibility of ground support, and air support was already overstretched dealing with three points of crisis – the battered and beleaguered ground convoy, still at that time battling through the streets of the city, and the two crash sites, the first, that of Super 61, reasonably static but highly

Soldiers from the 75th Ranger Regiment descend in an MH-6 Little Bird helicopter flown by pilots from the 160th Special Operations Aviation Regiment.

Chalk Four Rangers return to base after a mission in Somalia, 1993.

insecure, the second with mere moments to spare before being overrun.

A moment of profound human decision then followed. Providing sniper cover from the air were two Delta Force snipers, Sergeant First Class Randall 'Randy' Shughart and Master Sergeant Gary Gordon. The two submitted repeated requests to JOC to be dropped into Crash Site Two to help defend it from the large numbers of Somalis drawing in. In due course, permission was given and the two were inserted at a point some 100 metres from the crash site. Once on the scene, they extracted a badly wounded Durant from his pilot's seat, placing him in a position where he would be able to contribute to providing cover. They also attended, as much as possible, to the other crew members, and then fought to the death to defend the site. Only Durant survived, and after dreadful mistreatment at the hands of the Somalis, he was retained as a captive-hostage. Shugart and Gordon were both given a posthumous award of the Congressional Medal of Honour for their extraordinarily selfless and astonishingly courageous actions of that day.

Reports differ on exactly how long Gordon and Shughart were able to hold the crash site. According to one news report, the helicopter crew and two Delta snipers were able to hold the Somalis at bay for about two hours. Another report states that Shughart and Gordon were able to hold out for just 20 minutes. Bearing in mind the extraordinary efforts made by Task Force Ranger and the Quick Reaction Force to reach Crash Site Two, it seems unlikely that either would have been recalled before Crash Site Two was overrun, which tends to support the former theory.

In the meanwhile, Aidid and his military captains were apprised very quickly of the fiasco that was unfolding in the Black Sea. The audacity of the TF Ranger assault had been premised on the smooth execution of the operation, which the SNA leadership had recognized very early could easily be derailed by the shooting down of an air asset, preferably a crew-served Black Hawk. Just as it had been recognized that the Americans would not engage unarmed civilians, presenting the opportunity to use unarmed civilians as cover, the absurd battlefield morality that governed US action would serve to ensure that a downed aircraft would attract reinforcements, which, in turn, offered potential for even greater carnage.

And so it was. The Quick Reaction Force, although it was not directly integrated into the order of battle, had been notified a full hour ahead of the launch of the assault that an operation was pending, which was commonly the case, after which no further indication or information would typically be given.

However, at 15h37, a REDCON ONE alert was received at QRF headquarters from Task Force Ranger headquarters, amplifying the state of readiness, and hinting, for the first time, that Task Force Ranger might have tripped up. The QRF was located in the university grounds, some three miles from the airport.

Then, at 16h30, minutes after the shooting down of Super 61, came the call for the Quick Reaction Force to present itself at the airport, where it would be placed under the command of Task Force Ranger commander, General William Garrison.

News was already common that Cliff Wolcott's Super 61 had gone down, followed upon arrival at the airport, at 17h24, with the additional shocking news that Durant's Super 64 was also stricken somewhere on the edges of the Black Sea.

It was known that Ranger elements had already secured the first crash site, that a significant battle was underway to hold it, and that casualties had been taken and were continuing to be taken. The status of Crash Site Two was still uncertain. Gordon and Shughart were still alive and defending the position, but it was not anticipated that this could be sustained for much longer. The QRF column, commanded by Lieutenant-Colonel William David, was issued the unenviable and deceptively simple command to proceed from the airport grounds to secure Michael Durant's Crash Site Two. The convoy ran into immediate and heavy enemy action as it left the airport, meeting an improvised Task Force Ranger convoy racing in the other direction, fleeing the tempest of fire and steel that it too had sought to penetrate in response to the desperate situation at Crash Site Two. It had been ambushed almost from the moment it had left the security of the airport, and although coming within sight of the crash, was unable to break through. The Quick Reaction Force convoy, consisting again of Humvees and open five-ton trucks, was also unable to sustain any real forward momentum and fell back, returning to the airport precinct at about 19h00.

In the meanwhile, Montgomery had been mustering the Malaysians and Pakistanis, suddenly an extremely valuable asset with their combined tanks and armoured troop carriers. Almost as soon as he stepped out of his bullet-pocked vehicle, Lieutenant-Colonel David was apprised of a new plan involving two Malaysian APC companies and a Pakistani tank platoon. These, in the main, consisted of West German-made Condor APCs and US-made M-48 tanks.

OH-58D Kiowa and AH-64 Apache helicopters.

An MH-60L Black Hawk helicopter from Company D, 160th Special Operations Aviation Regiment (Airborne) flies low and fast.

This was the last resort, and an extremely difficult moment for the Task Force Ranger command. There had been no lack of inter-force rivalry and derision traded between the armies of different countries. The bulk of this had been directed mainly at Task Force Ranger by others in the theatre as a consequence of no small amount of professional arrogance and isolationism on the part of this elite grouping of soldiers, and the tendency of US forces, in general, to revel in the no-expense-spared nature of their equipment, training, support and command. It is also true that the Americans were quite often scathing towards the relatively humble capabilities of other armies, in particular those leanly equipped and modestly trained troops now mustering their archaic equipment to lend their weight to the extraction of Americans from a fiasco of their own making – or so to some it appeared. And certainly the American command could have drawn no pleasure from the admission implicit in all of this, that they were on their backs, and being viciously mauled by a rag-tag militia, barely trained, sparsely commanded and armed in the main with AK-47s and RPG rocket launchers. But, if the men besieged in the city were to be rescued, and some measure of credibility retrieved from the disaster, a plausible force had to be forged out these disparate units, using troops and commanders highly jittery about entering the tightening siege of the city, and with political masters extremely reluctant to risk committing troops to combat.

It is a credit, however, to the control and forbearance of all involved that a viable force was eventually put together, venturing out of the port area and into the ongoing maelstrom of fire at about 23h30 that evening, under the overall command of Lieutenant-Colonel David. The rescue force consisted of the Malaysians and Pakistanis, two quick-reaction force companies and a composite Ranger platoon made up of anyone and everyone willing to strap on armour, pick up a rifle and climb on board. There was a tangible lack of enthusiasm on the part of either the Pakistanis or the Malaysians to send troops or assets into the Bakaara Market area of Mogadishu, in particular in the midst of a deadly large-scale mobilization of hostile militias. This was the area that had been effectively abandoned by UN forces upon the departure of the US Marines. Italian and Indian armour was also in theatre, but it was the Pakistanis and Malaysians who were more immediately available and, as a consequence, they who came under enormous pressure to respond.

The 106-vehicle convoy began to take fire almost immediately, fighting its way slowly north up National Street towards an intersection where it was intended that the force would split up. From there, one detachment would head towards Crash Site Two and the other further north towards Crash Site One, where Ranger elements and surviving crew members were still engaged in an ongoing firefight and, by then, also protecting a large number of additional casualties.

Some confusion resulted in two APCs becoming detached from the main group, the lead vehicle being disabled by a direct RPG hit that also fatally wounded the driver. The QRF troops debussed and fought a tight defensive action for some time, before it was able to link up with the main column again, costing the lives of two Americans and one Malaysian.

In the meanwhile, the two crash sites were located, Durant's Crash Site Two quickly established as being without visible survivors, and destroyed, and the second still secured. Withdrawal from Crash Site One was delayed considerably as the body of pilot Cliff Wolcott was cut from the wreckage of the downed Super 61.

As dawn was rising over the smoke-filled capital, the column was finally able to begin its journey back to safety. The final drama belonged to a small detachment of Rangers left to run beside the cover of the retreating armoured vehicles, which, somewhat to their shame, made no attempt to maintain a compatible pace, but quickly left the Rangers exposed to run the distance to the Pakistani stadium unprotected, this becoming known as the infamous 'Mogadishu Mile'.

As an extremely sad postscript to the Battle of Mogadishu and Task Force Ranger, on Wednesday 6 October, two days after the battle, a single mortar round landed in the TF Ranger compound, injuring 13 soldiers, one of whom, SFC Mathew L. Reirson, a Delta operator from Nevada, Iowa, died of his injuries.

CHAPTER SIX: AND NOW WHAT?

Perhaps the most regrettable aspect of the entire international intervention in Somalia took place as the sun rose on the battle-scarred city of Mogadishu. As the crisis began with the memorable and shocking images, so it ended. These were not images of starving children, their paperlike skin pitched over skeletal bodies, but ostensibly those self-same people, the victims of yore, now dragging the bodies of slain US servicemen through the dusty streets of the capital. The corpses were accompanied by a baying, jeering mob of otherwise ordinary civilians, kicking and abusing those courageous sons of America, whose sole transgression, it seems, had been to attempt to save a nation from itself. In all, 18 US servicemen died that day, and 75 were injured, many seriously. Killed also were several hundred Somalis.

It goes without saying that the political fallout in the aftermath of the battle was considerable. Not least did the mantis-like secretary-general of the United Nations have the opportunity to say 'I told you so', but this bitter satisfaction must quickly have been tempered when news was delivered to him that a decision had been made to withdraw US troops altogether. The surge that followed was simply to protect those troops already in the theatre, and to more easily expedite a general withdrawal.

Among the warlords and the militant Somalis in general, there was a great deal of crowing over the defeat of a mighty superpower. In fact, the decision of the United States to throw in the towel had a more prosaic rationale, being premised simply on the fact that Somalia was of almost zero strategic value to the United States, and, in light of other ongoing and pending security issues – the war in the Balkans not least of these – Somalia could be left to stew in its own juices of violence and anarchy without noticeably impacting the evolution of the wider New World Order. The episode had been a valuable lesson in the unforeseen difficulties of intervention, which, sadly, would ramificate further into the decade with the explosion of ethnic violence that occurred in Rwanda the following year, into which situation the Clinton administration, notwithstanding being fully informed of the unfolding potential for genocide, opted not to intervene.

On 6 October, two days after the battle, President Bill Clinton convened an urgent policy review session that included Vice-President Al Gore, key cabinet members and senior civilian and military staff, including Robert Oakley. The result was a radically revised policy, and a date selected for the withdrawal of all US forces from Somalia. Clinton personally ordered the acting chairman of the Joint Chiefs of Staff, Admiral David E. Jeremiah, and CENTCOM commander, General Hoar, to desist from any further operations against Aidid in particular, the SNA in general and any other Somali faction, except in self-defence. Aidid, needless to say, recognized this as being a rare moment when violence would not be the preferred policy, and kept his guns silent, declaring a unilateral ceasefire as the inevitable process of disengagement was rolled out.

Clinton, in the meanwhile, made public this major change in direction, staunchly defending the overall US policy toward Somalia, but acknowledging, although taking no personal responsibility for the fact, that it had been a mistake for US forces to be drawn so deeply into a personalized and extremely costly quest to pluck Aidid out of the picture. To the extent that is was possible, Clinton washed his hands of the episode. In a May 1994 discussion with family members of the Rangers killed, he is reported to have express dismay that the operation was authorized and mounted after he had himself stated his preference for a diplomatic solution. This fact was revealed in an extremely thoughtful and insightful article published on 13 May 1994, by Michael R. Gordon, chief military correspondent with the *New York Times*, who revealed quite the extent to which US military officers had been divided over the raid that sparked the Battle of Mogadishu.

The appointment of Robert Oakley as special envoy underlined the Clinton administration's determination to now pursue a diplomatic solution and, as quixotic as it might seem, this was to be focused on political reconciliation involving all Somali factions. The decision to re-engage Oakley, in tandem with a massive force build-up, more or less signalled a return to the UNITAF policy of a big stick held in abeyance behind a substantial diplomatic carrot. The carrot, of course, was Oakley, who had, throughout, revealed himself as being as powerful a force in terms of solid achievement than anything else so far attempted in Somalia, military or civil. Needless to say, within a US military already somewhat jaded against Clinton, this turn of events did not sit well.

The extent to which there had been a disconnect at the highest level over the decision to specifically target Aidid was revealed during a hearing of the Senate Armed Services Committee early in May, during which, testimony was heard from a number of sources. Major-General Thomas Montgomery, while defending the effort to capture Aidid, did concede that 'military superiors in the United States had been dubious about the mission'.[10] According to chief military correspondent to the *New York Times*, Michael R. Gordon:

> In defending the effort to capture General Aidid, General Montgomery said that the United States had good intelligence on the Somali warlord and that the military assessment was that the capture of the Somali strongman was necessary to break the back of the Somali resistance thwarting the United Nations. In doing so, General Montgomery acknowledged, he differed with Gen. Joseph P. Hoar, the head of the United States Central Command, and Gen. Colin L. Powell, then Chairman of the Joint Chiefs of Staff.[11]

Also testifying was General William Garrison, whose principal point was the potential advantage that would have been gained during the crucial sequences of battle, if his request for AC-130 gunships had not been rejected – similarly the heavy armour – although Garrison did conceded that it is unlikely that he would have made use of armour during the original phases of the operation, but that it certainly would have expedited the rescue had this equipment been available. The fact that helicopter gunships were required to hover at an average of 100 feet above ground in order to direct their fire, made them extremely vulnerable targets, a risk that would not have been run by an AC-130 gunship, which would, in addition to the obvious physcological effect on the enemy, have simplified the response to the downed Black Hawks. In fact, it is probable that no helicopters would have been hit at all under cover of one or more AC-130s.

In the end, blame was laid at the feet of the United Nations, and those within the US administration who, at the time, had allowed themselves to be influenced by the world body in the decisions that were made pertaining to military preparedness in the Somalia theatre. Most frequently named were General Colin Powell himself, who appeared to obfuscate quite considerably, and secretary for defence, Les Aspin, both of whom seemed to concern themselves more with the appearance and political effect of too-overt a build-up of force in Somalia, while at the same time authorizing the use of what force did exist on the ground in a proactive manner.

In a senate report released in October 1995, a great deal of space was taken up with various criticisms related to the decision not to send AC-130 gunships as part of the force package, a decision that almost completely informs a book by Colonel Danny McKnight, *Streets of Mogadishu*, in which he examines the leadership successes and failures of the operation, referring frequently to Stupid Decisions at a command level with barely disguised anger and venom. The senate report was authored by two senior members of the Senate Armed Services Committee, senators John Warner and Carl Levin, who commented thus: 'The AC-130s were part of all the force package options and were included in all of the training exercises. This decision is inconsistent with the principle that you fight as you train.' AC-130s had, in fact, been deployed, and used, in recent UNOSOM actions in Somalia, but the excess of collateral damage prompted a redeployment. This was seen by Aidid as a victory, and, thanks to the 'CNN' factor, there was a reluctance at a command level to redeploy it back into the theatre.

Les Aspin, oddly, in the midst of much general criticism, suffered censure for poor risk assessment in the light of the number of similar operations conducted prior to 3 October, and for not alerting General Garrison to both the policy shift toward a political solution and the enhanced risk of tactical predictability.

> Had Aspin either reassessed the risk of each TFR operation more thoroughly or done a better job coordinating the policy shift in light of the increased risks, it is likely that the 3 October raid would not have occurred.[12]

From the view of a layman, this would seem to be grossly unfair, bearing in mind that Aspin was a civilian and Garrison a seasoned military professional who, of all parties involved, should have been aware of the practical risks, and should have instinctively embraced the danger of repeating the same tactics more than once. In a situation where US troops were so enormously outnumbered, relying as a consequence on lightning speed and surprise – and, moreover, bearing in mind that Somalis with even rudimentary communication would be aware within minutes of the launch that a raid was underway, and if it could be predicted what form the raid would take, RPGs would quite naturally be strategically deployed with a view to targeting the helicopters, which would almost inevitably be in low orbit over the target area.

Aspin, however, appeared to take the fall for all of this, and other failed aspects of the Clinton administration's foreign policy. He resigned for personal reasons later that year, and died soon afterward of a heart attack. However, quite obviously the fiasco of 3 October cannot be blamed entirely on one man's fumbling of key security decisions. The failure was multi-faceted, and can be traced from the highest decision-making level, through the chain of command, all the way down to a basic tactical level. On a strategic level it was a failure of state policy, on a command level it was a failure of generals and securocrats to prioritize military concerns over political, and on a tactical level it was a failure to anticipate and adapt.

The Battle of Mogadishu has, in fact, never been acknowledged as a defeat, which in strict terms it was not. The objective was achieved and all troops were returned. This, however, does not detract from the fact that it did precede the collapse of UNOSOM, which handed Aidid a *de facto* victory that he could not claim on the battlefield. There are no accurate figures as to how many Somali fighters and civilians died during the battle, with estimates ranging between 300 and 1,000 killed and many more wounded. Aidid was severely rattled by the events of 3/4 October and was closer to compromise in its aftermath than at any time hitherto.

From a military point of view, it is the analysis of the lack of adaptability on a tactical level that is the most interesting aspect of the general failure. The first point worth noting is that the local and central military command, the latter responding in part to political concerns, suffered a critical communication disconnect. The Clinton administration assumed office without a coherent plan for Somalia. Initially, a purely military solution was sought, but, in due course, this evolved into a policy of military containment and pressure, while a political solution was sought. This fact was not communicated to the men on the ground. It is conceivable that had Major-General Garrison been aware that Aidid's value as a target had diminished, the Battle of Mogadishu would not have taken place at all. This, perhaps arguably, is where Les Aspin certainly can be held to fault.

It is perhaps worth mentioning here that the main force behind the deployment of Task Force Ranger for the purpose of capturing Aidid was an extension of a policy first established by retired Admiral Jonathan Howe, UN special representative, who had initially driven that policy with what UN forces had been available to him and, upon realizing that this was impossible, he lobbied hard among friends and connections in Washington for the deployment of Delta Force, which Clinton conceded to, upon the killing of US servicemen by improvised explosive devices and landmines. Ironically then, no sooner had the fateful 3 October operation begun than Howe arrived in the skies over Mogadishu, returning from Djibouti and Addis Ababa where he had been party to efforts to find a way of diplomatically dealing with Aidid. At this point, it was recognized, at least on a political level, that Aidid was willing to negotiate. He had earlier contacted Jimmy Carter, expressing an earnest desire for the veteran diplomat to intervene on his behalf by means of an independent commission, going as far as to propose a negotiated solution to his stand-off with the United Nations. Carter presented this approach to Clinton, who received it warmly. It seems strange, then, that since this was the understood situation, and Howe, the very man who had brought in the posse, was abroad presenting a diplomatic face to US and UN policy, that at precisely the same time, Task Force Ranger was tearing up Mogadishu in an aggressive search for Aidid.

However, Garrison was working with what he had. Putting aside any possible result that could have been achieved had there been American armour and additional air support available, most battlefield analyses conclude that Garrison had what he needed available to him to successfully execute various operations, but that the allocation of those resources was where his failure lay. Garrison had accepted upon the launch of Operation Gothic Serpent the removal from the initial Task Force Ranger strength of one Ranger platoon, again for the sake of political appearances, on the understanding that the Quick Reaction Force would be available for security back-up and reinforcement as and when required. Very little, if any, coordination was undertaken between the two units in order to successfully integrate them and, in fact, the Quick Reaction Force had been kept more or less out of the loop – informed on a superficial level, certainly – but by no means regarded or treated as a necessary adjunct to Task Force Rangers' capabilities.

At a command level, it seems that General Hoar shouldered the greatest responsibility for failing to ensure a unity of effort between Garrison and Montgomery. Under the Goldwater-Nichols Act of 1986, he alone had the authority to ensure a coordination of effort between Task Force Ranger and the Quick Reaction Force. There was, however, a number of command and control anomalies throughout the UNOSOM II period. The logistical components of US forces in Somalia were under the operational control of the United Nations in the person of Montgomery, while the Quick Reaction Force was commanded and controlled by CENTCOM. Task Force Ranger occupied a third command and control chain. Much of this was configured to ensure that US forces remained strictly under US command.

Had the Quick Reaction Force been on immediate standby at the airport, and not several miles away at the university compound, it would have been available and ready to deploy immediately to secure Crash Site Two before the Somalis were in a position to react. What is more, the Quick Reaction Force would have been even better equipped had Aspin approved the deployment of four M1 tanks and 14 M2 infantry fighting vehicles as had been requested by Montgomery. However, the fact that the Quick Reaction Force was not included in any Task Force Ranger contingency planning would, in practical terms, have limited the usefulness of these assets, even had they been available.

The fact is that US armour was not available, so a better coordination with other forces in the theatre, the Pakistanis and Malaysians in particular, would have resulted in a much speedier and efficient deployment of what armour was available in the event of a catastrophe of this nature. Furthermore, the deployment of a single combat search and rescue team implied the expectation that, at the very most, one combat search and rescue scenario was all that could conceivably occur. And, bearing in mind the fact that the air was filled with low-flying air traffic, and that the Somalis had quite evidently digested the vulnerably of helicopters to coordinated RPG fire, planning for the operation appears to have assumed only a best-case scenario.*

* A week earlier, a 10th Mountain Division UH-60 had been shot down by a Somali RPG while flying at 130 knots, at rooftop level and at night; and during the sixth TFR raid on 21 September 1993, that captured Osman Atto, about 15 RPGs had fired on TFR helicopters. Clearly this implied that the Somalis were targeting helicopters.

This highlights the failure of Task Force Ranger to plan an operation that adequately protected its tactical decisive point – its helicopters. The most vulnerable of these were the relatively slow-moving Black Hawks, which remained in close orbit and within RPG range for 40 minutes after the initial deployment of the assault force on the target building.[13] Initially, there would not appear to have been any reason to use the UH-60s in a troop support role, with a more sensible approach being to move the heavier helicopters out of range of ground fire soon after the drop-off, relying more on the faster and lighter MH-6 and AH-6 Little Birds using miniguns and snipers to provide ground support. Even after Super 61 had gone down, and despite there being only one CSAR team available, UH-60s remained in the area supporting ground forces despite the fact that Little Birds were available.

Perhaps the worst lapse, however, was the lack of recognition at the JOC level that the Somalis were capable of shooting down, and were, in fact, actively targeting, helicopters. According to Mark Bowden, who wrote the definitive history of the Battle of Mogadishu in his book *Black Hawk Down*:

> The QRF Black Hawk that had gone down the week before had been hit by an RPG. It had burst into flames on impact. That incident started everybody rethinking the way they had been doing things, even though the task force's six missions had gone without a hitch. Some of the pilots began agitating for more flexibility, but their commanders wanted them to stick to the template.[14]

If this was so, then Garrison is certainly guilty of tactical inflexibility. His belief was, not unjustly, that the downing of the Quick Reaction Force Black Hawk, Courage 53, had been a lucky shot, which it was, bearing in mind that it was a moonless portion of the morning (02h00) and the aircraft was flying without lights. The Quick Reaction Force HQ had earlier received indications that the SNA might deliberately be targeting helicopters – creating incidents to lure observation helicopters before attacking them from all sides with RPGs.

CHAPTER SEVEN: BUILD-UP AND WITHDRAWAL

This is one of the most schizophrenic acts in recent history. It strikes me as strange to tell American troops to hunt him [Aidid] one day and chauffeur him around the next
– Senator Hank Brown

Whatever might have been underway in the corridors of power, on the ground in Mogadishu neither the commanders nor rank and file of any force anticipated that the events of 3 October would result in a complete reversal of the current strategy. The men of Task Force Ranger, more than any other, were eager for an early rematch with the SNA militias. So also was the UN command. Within hours of the safe extraction of Task Force Ranger personnel from the city, UN commander, Lieutenant-General Cevik Bir contacted Admiral Howe in a state of some

US Navy admiral, David E. Jeremiah, vice-chairman of the Joint Chiefs of Staff

Headquarters staff, 43rd Corps Support Group (now 43rd Sustainment Brigade)

excitement, reiterating that Mogadishu was the centre of gravity for the whole operation, and Aidid the principal bogey. He urged that the focus of operations should continue in Mogadishu, and pressure on Aidid retained.

There was a great deal of logic in this assessment of the situation. Aidid's position at that time was indeed precarious. The battle had been a great deal more costly for the SNA than it had been for Task Force Ranger. The numbers of Somali dead ran into the hundreds, with over 1,000 wounded. And while this might not have been expected to personally move him, it had generated considerable anger among the members of his clan and clan affiliates whose family members had died, which naturally tended to unsettle the delicate balance of his own coalition. Another fact was the expectation among his key supporters that the Americans would quickly regroup and return to unequivocally make the point of their military superiority, which prompted many militiamen to simply decamp and flee the city. Moreover, the battle had depleted Aidid's stockpiles of ordnance, and he could now not afford a second open brawl with the Americans, particularly as the air space over Mogadishu was suddenly lit up with US air traffic, implying reinforcement and re-equipping on a scale that he could hardly match. He had retained one ace up his sleeve during the entire UNOSOM II period, and it had been played, and now there was nothing more.

The decision to withdraw was not made on a tactical level, but in Washington, based primarily on political considerations. An incredulous military establishment digested, with dismay, the expectation that, after the loss of life and the humiliation of baying crowds dragging dead US servicemen through the streets of Mogadishu, that the most powerful military in the world was ostensibly caving in and fleeing the battle. Bearing in mind Aidid's vulnerability, the opportunity to fully exploit the military situation in the capital seemed more immediately attractive than re-igniting a political dialogue. Aidid was on his back, so it was quite obviously the time to deliver a well-aimed kick.

For Montgomery, deputy commander of UN forces in Somalia, and commander of US forces, and to Admiral Howe to some extent, the decision came as something of a personal embarrassment. During the course of UNOSOM II, both men had found it necessary to coax often reluctant coalition partners to undertake risky missions, which was complicated by the fact that foreign unit commanders had habitually sought clearance from national governments before accepting any assignments.* One of these had been the Pakistanis, who had lost 40 of their members to Aidid's militia, and yet they had remained in theatre, and moreover, had committed men and equipment for the rescue of American troops in an extremely dangerous situation. Now, having suffered a relatively small number of casualties, political direction from Washington was that US troops would be pulled out, precisely what the US had, in effect, been criticizing others for doing, or wanting to do.

> To many within UNOSOM II, President Clinton's decision broke faith with those coalition units that had taken casualties but stayed the course. Prior to 7 October, Montgomery had often found it aggravating the degree to which foreign governments directed the activities of their military forces in Somalia. Now, to his chagrin, his own government had become a source of that aggravation, to be weighed in with 'the almost daily decisions of coalition partners to revisit their national commitments to the mission' in the light of Washington's shift in policy.[15]

This, in essence, implied that, after goading its coalition partners for being scaredy cats, it was the US that was the first to flee the theatre the moment that it was given a bloody nose. None of this sat well with the men of Task Force Ranger, then preparing to leave the theatre, and certainly not a military establishment already extremely uncomfortable with the Clinton administration.

That notwithstanding, the die had been cast, and when Oakley arrived in Mogadishu on 9 October, less than a week after the battle, his primary objective was to secure the release of Michael Durant, and a Nigerian soldier also in captivity, and to claim the

* The commander of the Italian contingent, with the full approval of his government, was reported to have opened separate negotiations with the fugitive Aidid. The UN requested the officer's relief from command for insubordination, which the Italian government refused to do.

US Marines perform pre-mission checks on an M1A1 Abrams tank.

bodies of the TF Ranger members still unaccounted for.* It was on that very day that Aidid emerged very briefly from hiding to hold a press conference, during which he proclaimed his unilateral ceasefire, making, some would have said, a virtue out of a necessity. Bir and Montgomery scoffed at the mere suggestion of Aidid driving the terms of peace, still rankling at their inability to finish the job. It was not they who required a ceasefire, they grumbled, but Aidid himself.

Oakley, meanwhile, re-established contacts with the right people and was very quickly talking through intermediaries to both Ali Mahdi and Aidid, urging a stronger and more inclusive political dialogue, a consolidation of the ceasefire and support for the influence of moderate, or 'sensible' Somalis.[16]

He then put the case for the immediate and unconditional release of Durant and the captured Nigerian soldier, startling the Somalis with the simple insistence that the US president wanted the release of the two men, Durant in particular, immediately and unconditionally. Bearing in mind that a large number of influential Somalis languished in captivity in a temporary camp on an island off the port city of Kismayo, among them Osman Atto, captured during TF Ranger's sixth operation, this was a lot to expect. The obvious hope among Somalis had been that a deal would be done for a prisoner exchange, but Oakley, very sure of his ground, pointed out two things: the first was that the United States did not negotiate over matters of hostages or prisoners, and secondly, that a failure to release the captured Black Hawk pilot would result in a search and rescue operation. Mark Bowden, in his excellent and highly detailed account of the Battle of Mogadishu, *Black Hawk Down*, relates a snippet of dialogue attributed to Oakley, that is possibly somewhat dramatized, but which, nonetheless, makes the point very clearly:

> I have no plan for this, but I'll do everything I can to prevent it, but what will happen if a few weeks go by and Mr Durant is not released? Not only will you lose any credit that you might get now, but we will decide that we have to rescue him. I guarantee you we are not going to pay or trade for him in any way, shape or form. So what we'll decide is we have to rescue him, and whether we have the right place or the wrong place, there's going to be a fight with your people. The minute the guns start again, all restraint on the US side goes. Just look at the stuff coming in here now. An aircraft carrier, tanks, gunships ... the works. Once the fighting starts, all of this pent-up anger is going to be released. This whole part of the city will be destroyed, men, women, children, camels, cats, dogs, goats, donkeys, everything.[17]

This certainly was fighting talk, and somewhat out of character for the gaunt, taciturn Oakley who had returned to the city without direct advice to offer, but certainly with little obvious enthusiasm for the hawkish attitudes of the incumbent military command. And yet, the fact remained that the little Somali dog had certainly given the large American dog a painful nip on the ankle, and could expect a vicious mauling in reply if certain acts of contrition were not offered up quickly and sincerely. And with the prompt and massive build-up of military force underway, there could be little doubt that Oakley was sincere in the advice that he offered.

In the meanwhile, Michael Durant's personal circumstances had improved somewhat since those awful and frantic moments when Crash Site Two was overrun and his comrades slain. His injuries had been modestly treated and he was being held in reasonably comfortable conditions. His initial capture had been terrifying and chaotic and, bearing in mind the known propensity of the Somalis for mutilation and torture, he had no reason to suppose that he would not be killed. His initial rescue had been by a local neighbourhood militia leader who then attempted to remove him from the city for the purpose of demanding a ransom. The effort was intercepted by a stronger group, and Durant was essentially stolen at gunpoint, and then sold for ransom to Aidid himself.

Aidid would have done this for obvious reasons, and was presumably extremely disappointed with the conditions that Oakley defined for his release. He recognized, however, that he had very little choice in the matter and, after understandably difficult consultations within his faction – particularly in regard to those with relatives still held by the United Nations – it was

* Oakley returned in the company of General Anthony Zinni.

A demonstration in ordnance disposal is conducted by French soldiers from the Military Instruction Advisory Detachment (IMAD) of the 5th Regiment International Army Overseas (RIAOM). The French provided training for the Somali police in Baidoa and Buurhakaba.

agreed that Durant and Nigerian Umar Shantali would be released on 14 October. Oakley, with undiminished diplomatic cachet, allowed Aidid to emerge from hiding in order to announce the planned release himself. In partial recognition of this, Aidid was rewarded with a suspension of the UN approval of his arrest when Resolution 885 was debated and passed in the Security Council on 16 October, two days after Durant's release. In addition, Security Council Resolution 885 authorized a commission to look into the events of 5 June which resulted in the deaths of 24 Pakistani soldiers. It was two months, however, before Boutros-Ghali conceded to the release of eight people, including Osman Atto, still being held by UN forces for real or suspected sympathies with the SNA.

As promised, Durant was handed over to Red Cross officials with a minimum of ceremony. The men of Task Force Ranger were waiting for Durant when he returned to the airport. A corridor was formed from the base driveway to the platform of the transport aircraft ready to fly the injured pilot to Germany. The Ranger creed of no man left behind had been fulfilled. On 17 October, the men of Task Force Ranger decamped from Somalia aboard a flight of C-5 transports, leaving as they had arrived, with a minimum of fanfare. All that remained was a handful of sandbagged aircraft revetments and an empty aircraft hangar. A few days earlier, General William Garrison had sent a hand-written letter to President Bill Clinton, accepting full responsibility for the events of 3 October.[18]

Behind the scenes the massive build-up of force continued. A fairly arbitrary deadline of 31 March 1994 had been set for the withdrawal of US forces from Somalia, which quite naturally had a domino effect among other coalition partners with troops in the country. Other governments, mainly Italy, Germany and Turkey, also opted to remove their troops from Somalia, effectively rendering UNOSOM II impotent to carry out its mandate. Patrols in Mogadishu were limited to areas supportive of UN activities, while it was formally communicated to the warlords that UNOSOM II would remain neutral in any inter-clan friction that might erupt in the city – good news for Aidid, but something of an abandonment of Ali Mahdi and his faction that had placed significant reliance on UN support. The first serious clash of this nature took place on 25 October when militiamen of Aidid's and Ali Mahdi's factions battled along the green line, resulting in the deaths of ten Somalis and 40 wounded.

UNOSOM II activities reverted more or less to a Chapter VI peacekeeping role, which, in the UN context, implied a presence but nothing more, as opposed to the more aggressive Chapter VII peace-enforcement role. Troops in the capital tended to regress to a garrison mindset and a general military paralysis pervaded. Generals Bir and Montgomery, meanwhile, had their hands full dealing with the large numbers of US troops and quantities of equipment flooding into the theatre.

The first to arrive touched down on 8 October, the day after the announcement of the shift in US policy, and a day before the arrival of Robert Oakley. This was a mechanized company of the 24th Infantry Division that would form part of a battalion task force, designated TF 1-64, including two platoons equipped with Bradley fighting vehicles and one platoon of Abrams tanks. The balance of the task force began to arrive a few days later, accompanied by the 43rd Combat Engineer Battalion, a battalion of the 10th Mountain Division, four AC-130 gunships and various Marine and naval units which appeared off the coast, including the carrier battle group of the USS *Abraham Lincoln*. And just to make the point that the heavy linebackers had arrived on the field, on 10 October an AC-130 assault was ordered against a redundant weapons cache located north of Mogadishu. The following day, aircraft from the *Abraham Lincoln* began to mount high-profile reconnaissance sorties over the UNOSOM II area of responsibility.

The main point of vulnerability lay both with the volume of heavy transport aircraft traffic moving in and out of the airport and the numbers of aircraft parked within the secure perimeter. The former were vulnerable to surface-to-air missiles which were known to be in the hands of the SNA, and the latter to artillery or mortar attack which, if successful, would have closed the airport for a long time. The US, however, had stated its deadline for the removal of its troops and it would have made little sense for Aidid to antagonize the Americans and prompt a delay, so the opportunity for mayhem was never availed upon.

In the meanwhile, once the force build-up was complete, the US presence inside Somalia had effectively doubled to over 4,300, with an additional 9,100 located offshore. Attached to the Quick Reaction Force were 3,500 troops in six battalions. The QRF was renamed the Falcon Brigade under the command of Colonel Lawrence Casper of the 10th Mountain Division's 10th Aviation Brigade.

It is perhaps worthwhile here to briefly trace the evolution of the 10th Mountain Division's journey through the Somali crisis. Command of the QRF had been assumed by Colonel Lawrence Casper just three days before the battle of 3 October, which, at the very least, was a prompt rite of passage for a highly accomplished and technical soldier coming to grips with the command and control anomalies of the Somali theatre. The fact, for example, that as commanding officer of the Quick Reaction Force, Casper was not involved in or made aware of the Task Force Ranger planning for the mission until it began to run into trouble, was an early indication of the confused nature of the Somalia situation.

With the shift of responsibility from UNITAF to UNOSOM II earlier in the year, the 10th Mountain Division presence in Somalia allowed for a smooth transfer of the heavy-support role for UN operations in the country to this force, then named the Quick Reaction Force, or QRF. The initial proposal for a QRF had envisaged a combat brigade, located offshore, to provide a mailed fist to back up the essentially symbolic UN force, with responsibility for this role passed on to one of the contributing nations onshore when that became possible. The force would be positioned to provide a rapid-reaction force only when specific threats, attacks or other such emergencies exceeded the capacity of regular UNOSOM II forces to deal with them. In practical terms, as was the case with the 5 June incident, this could mean any kind of threatening situation at all. The force was expressively prohibited from spearheading everyday operations, those being routine patrolling, escorting convoys or providing long-term security. Command of the Quick Reaction Force was the responsibility of General Montgomery as commander of US Forces Somalia (USFORSOM), but without adequate US staff at his disposal, the planning for QRF operations devolved to the QRF staff itself, which was on the whole ill equipped for this level of planning.[19]

Colonel Lawrence Casper, of the 10th Mountain 10th Aviation Brigade, has contributed to the large body of analytical literature available on the US/Somalia relationship between 1992 and 1994, with, perhaps, one of the better-observed of many books written. *Falcon Brigade, Combat and Command in Somalia and Haiti* details the experience of the Falcon Brigade in both theatres, the one more or less leading into the other, and both not without similarities. As he familiarized himself with his command, Casper was intially struck by the lack of liaison and communication with Task Force Ranger, then in the midst of the hunt for Aidid, and still registering tactical successes, even though the main prize remained elusive. According to Casper as he toured the QRF operation's centre:

> I was astounded by the complete lack of information. We were reinforcements for every US and UN force in the theatre, and we didn't know what was occurring in our backyard.[20]

The ultimate result of this disinclination on the part of the Task Force Ranger command to include the Quick Reaction Force in its detailed planning has been discussed. Major-General William Garrison has suffered no small amount of criticism as a result of this, and he, later, in a hand-written note to President Bill Clinton, accepted full responsibility for this and all the failures of that day, which, of course, is the least to be expected of a man in his position, of his calibre and with his command responsibilities.

Interestingly, Colonel Lawrence Casper represented the 10th Mountain 10th Aviation Brigade, and, as such, symbolized what was really an unusual state of affairs. The core of the aviation brigade headquarters was deployed to Somalia on 27 July 1993, where, on 7 August, it assumed command of the QRF mission from the 10th Mountain's 2nd Infantry Brigade headquarters. This represented the first time that ground-manoeuvre forces had been placed under the direct command of an aviation headquarters during combat operations. According to Casper:

> Since the inception of the army's aviation branch in 1983, aviation leadership had touted the aviation brigade headquarters as the division commander's fourth manoeuvre headquarters, attempting to place it on an equal footing with the infantry and armour manoeuvre brigades. Our doctrine supported the use of aviation headquarters in this manner, and some commands exercised their fourth manoeuvre headquarters during division, field and command post training.[21]

This did not sit well with many officers who argued that the headquarters lacked resources, had a minimal depth and was without certain key staff functions. An aviation brigade, it was argued, could not be expected to be familiar with the organizational peculiarities, weapons and tactics of an infantry fighting force, and nor did it possess either the fully functional fire-support element nor the specific engineering assets required by an infantry brigade. Casper goes on to quote an interesting snippet from Lieutenant-Colonel Daniel P. Bolger's 1995 study of the strengths and limitations of US military capacity, *Savage Peace: Americans at War in the 1990s*, clearly written from the side of the sceptics:

> An aviation brigade is not organized or structured as well as other types of manoeuvre brigades for the command and control of what is, predominantly, a ground-manoeuvre force. Soldiers knew this. But 1st and 2nd Brigades had just done their turns. So, as the books say, 10 Mountain 'accepted risk' and put pilots in charge of riflemen.[22]

For the most part, however, planning and operations at that point revolved around nothing more than greeting and accommodating large numbers of incoming troops and, with the changes underway, came a restructuring of command. Joint Task Force Somalia was commanded by Major-General Carl F. Ernst, in charge of one of 'the most schizophrenic acts in recent history' – a gargantuan military operation that tried to determine some operational purpose for itself, but, in the end, amounted to nothing more than an impressive rearguard action. The last thing to leave, according to a sardonic comment made by General Montgomery, would be an Abrams tanks with its gun tube pointed toward Mogadishu.[23]

Joint Task Force Somalia was activated as a consequence of the determination of Washington to ensure that all forces entering Somalia as a consequence of the 7 October policy statement would remain under US command. Joint Task Force Somalia functioned as a headquarters under CENTCOM, which would exercise operational control of all incoming US forces, as well as those already in Somalia. Ernst was named commander, and given by General Hoar essentially a three-point set of instructions: to protect US forces, support the UN, and keep lines of communication open, the latter point being essentially to reopen the roads of Mogadishu and keep them open.

A commonly applied military maxim states that, while amateurs talk strategy, professionals talk logistics, and one thing that the armed forces of the United States have in recent years developed into a fine art is the organization of massive logistical manoeuvre in an austere operational environment. According to US defence analyst, Colonel Kenneth Allard, who authored a revealing study of US operations in Somalia entitled, *Somalia Operations: Lessons Learned*:

> What is clear, especially from the record of our support to UNOSOM II, is that management of theatre-level combat service support in an austere environment is something in which we excel.[24]

The winding-down of US operations in Somalia certainly bore this point out. Aside from the basic elements of force protection – primarily the key UN bases of Sword and Hunter, each vulnerably located and poorly protected – General Ernst concerned himself with establishing and streamlining the Joint Task Force Somalia HQ. He had equipped himself with a small but efficient staff, with, at its nucleus, personnel from the 10th Mountain Division, with additional support provided by liaison officers sent to his HQ by those components over which he enjoyed operational control. These were the Falcon Brigade, a joint special operations task force (JSOTF), and a psychological operations task force (POTF). Over the Marine and navy components positioned offshore, Ernst exercised only tactical control, which required a series of informal gentlemen's agreements to make a working relationship work. This was augmented by the addition of various liaison teams that all helped to support the intrinsic capabilities of JTF Somalia, as well as to quickly expedite the flow of orders and information back and forth. Once fully constituted, General Ernst's staff consisted of 80 per cent army personnel and ten percent Marine.

Ernst then sought to familiarize himself with the nuances of the situation on the ground. Information was available to him from a number of sources, one of which was General Garrison prior to his departure, which, operationally, was of enormous value, and politically from the Oakley–Zinni partnership, whose views he found himself most naturally aligned with. The opposing camp was represented by the UN military leadership in the persons of Montgomery and Bir, who had suffered a certain amount of criticism from Oakley and Zinni, criticism that rubbed off on Ernst, which, in turn, set the tone for a less than friendly relationship and a non-convergence of the differing threads of command and control in the theatre.

Through Oakley, Ernst was also able to communicate directly to Aidid and Mahdi regarding his minimum expectations during the withdrawal process that was underway – which was essential to the removal of roadblocks, the freeing-up of lines of communication and the free movement of UN convoys. Should either warlord fail to comply with all of this, it was advised that the additional US deployed forces would ensure that they did.

Beyond this, Ernst did not attempt to replicate the level of involvement with the political process that Lieutenant-General Johnston had sought during the UNITAF phase, and nor did Joint Task Force Somalia involve itself too closely with the work and requirements of the humanitarian organizations, adhering, more or less, strictly to the principal mission of providing force protection to US forces.

Perhaps more importantly than Ernst's easy rapport with Oakley, and more immediately impactful, was the unsuccessful meeting of minds experienced between him and Montgomery as the two principal US military personalities in the theatre. On a broad level, both were in agreement regarding the situation in Somalia and the overall mission. Montgomery, who worked with a small staff within the UN Logistics Support Command, welcomed the more robust planning capacity of the Joint Task Force, acknowledging that UN forces, in general, had developed a bunker mentality, essentially paralyzed, and he agreed with the principle that any transgression on the part of either warlord would be met with a vigorous response.

There their agreement ended. Relations between the two men were fractious from the outset. There was little in practical terms that could account for this, other than the overarching sense on the part of Montgomery, and, to a lesser extent, Cevic Bir, that they had been on the ground throughout the dark days of UNOSOM II and could claim a better understanding of the military situation that Ernst who had just arrived and who had been immediately indoctrinated by the Oakley/Zinni position on the UNOSOM II response. It appeared that Ernst sought to run things with little or no regard to the broader perspective offered by the military men on the ground.

Oakley's position, inasmuch as it was incompatible with

A view of the port city of Merca in southern Somalia.

Montgomery's position, was that the political and diplomatic advances that had been made during UNITAF, the structures put in place and the relationships cultivated, had been subverted to an increasingly robust military response that had naturally escalated, resulting in a return to virtual anarchy on the streets of Mogadishu, and, to an extent, elsewhere in the country too.

Montgomery and other officers on the UN side of the US staff tended to suspect that Ernst would ultimately attempt to circumvent and marginalize USFORSOM and the UN forces command staff, which, to some extent, would inevitably occur if genuine enmity were to exist between the two commanders, and if, at the same time, there existed a lack of clear command and control guidelines subordinating one to the other.

Practically speaking, Montgomery, as the commander of US forces Somalia, remained under the operational control of the commander-in-chief, US Central Command (CINCCENT). As such, he exercised only tactical control (TACON) over JTF Somalia, which allowed him to offer Ernst specific, local direction on tactical operations, and Ernst was responsible to him for the planning and execution of tactical operations in Somalia. Montgomery, however, was unable to formally issue orders to Ernst except under certain specific circumstances. Despite this, Montgomery understood from discussions with CINCCENT that JTF Somalia had been established with its robust staff for the purpose of relieving COMUSFORSOM and US members of the UNOSOM II staff of the burden of tactical command and control of US combat forces. This, in turn, would allow Montgomery and his staff to focus on the operational level and the deployment of UN force.

Thus Montgomery took the view that General Hoar continued to exercise operational control (OPCON) over all US forces through COMUSFORSOM, counterbalanced somewhat by Ernst's alternate view.* Ernst was formally under the operational control of CINCCENT, and except in those instances where he was required to answer to Montgomery, he intended to make use of his direct channel to CENTCOM whenever he considered it necessary. This led to comments that the actual relationship between JTF Somalia and USFORSOM was 'more than TACON but less than OPCON'.[25]

Practically speaking, Ernst's priority was to get JTF Somalia up and running. The self-sustaining element of the operation was described very well by Ernst who commented that planning became the hallmark of the JFT staff. This planning translated into joint training that consumed a great deal of time and energy, tending, after a while, to look like a large show of force. According to Colonel Casper:

> Under the direction of JFT headquarters, we began working on a series of contingency plans to regain control of lost lines of communication (supply and transportation routes). Along with the planning, came a number of training exercises, followed by mission rehearsals. Major-General Ernst was the energy behind these initiatives. The operations brought to bear the tremendous combined-arms capability and firepower to the brigade.[26]

Casper also makes note of routine operations in support of UNOSOM II. A battalion strike force, comprising infantry, armour and aviation, was maintained and exercised, with its

* Joint Publication (JP) 1, Doctrine of the Armed Forces of the United States: OPCON is the command authority that may be exercised by CDRs at any echelon at or below the level of combatant command and may be delegated within the command. When forces are transferred between combatant commands, the command relationship the gaining CDR will exercise (and the losing CDR will relinquish) over these forces must be specified by the SecDef. OPCON is inherent in COCOM and is the authority to perform those functions of command over subordinate forces, involving organizing and employing commands and forces, assigning tasks, designating objectives, and giving authoritative direction necessary to accomplish the mission. OPCON includes authoritative direction over all aspects of military operations and joint training necessary to accomplish missions assigned to the command. TACON is the command authority over assigned or attached forces or commands, or military capability or forces made available for tasking, that is limited to the detailed direction and control of movements or manoeuvres within the operational area necessary to accomplish assigned missions or tasks. TACON is inherent in OPCON and may be delegated to and exercised by CDRs at any echelon at or below the level of combatant command. When forces are transferred between CDRs, the command relationship the gaining CDR will exercise (and the losing CDR will relinquish) over those forces must be specified by the SecDef.

USNS *Denebola* (T-AKR-289) docked at the port of Mogadishu, awaiting loading of US troops and equipment for redeployment back to the United States, February 1994.

headquarters rotated among the three ground-manoeuvre battalions. Conducting convoy exercises, manning and improving compound perimeters and securing the main supply routes, all of which were daily and routine activities. An interesting point to make here is that the main supply route from Mogadishu into the interior was via a bypass road that skirted Mogadishu to the west, a road that had been constructed by the UN to avoid the city. This was in respect of the fact that the established arterial routes through Mogadishu itself had for some time been untenable as a consequence of the general insecurity pervading, and the inability of the UN to impact that.

Larger operations did take place. The first of these was Operation Show Care which took place at the end of October and was undertaken to secure the coastal settlement of Merca, immediately southwest of Mogadishu, as a show of force and to secure the main road between Mogadishu and Kismayo. Forces used were elements of the 13th Marine Expeditionary Unit (SOC), deployed to conduct an amphibious and heliborne landing in the town, where they then linked up with the UNOSOM II unit holding the settlement, the Royal Moroccan Task Force. A general show of force followed, along with security operations and general civic projects.

A much more ambitious joint amphibious operation was launched early in November to similarly introduce JTF Somalia and its capabilities to Mogadishu. Not only was this a massive display of force, but it was also a working template for how the various command and control elements could be brought together in a single operation. The operation involved every section of JTF Somalia, and many of the command anomalies were dealt with informally, and overcome. One means by which Ernst was able to evade the unwieldy command and control requirements associated with actual operations was to label certain undertakings as training. In Ernst's own words:

> We ran a major operation in Mogadishu about the beginning of November 1993. This operation probably did the most to quiet the neighborhood of any single action we took. It was a joint amphibious operation in which every piece of the Joint Task Force participated. We brought one MEU ashore and then embarked an army mech/tank company team on LCACs that came in on the second wave. A Marine battalion landing team came into the old port area. They established a presence there and operated in the vicinity for three or four days. The Army task force brought in two mech company teams, leaving one at the airport and the other at the new port, then established a reserve force ashore. We positioned artillery throughout the area to provide fire support if needed. That gave us the Copperhead capture angles we needed to shoot into Mogadishu if it became necessary. The artillery fired out to sea for precise registration that night and it was a max sortie day over Mogadishu for carrier and other aircraft, including the AC-130s. We conducted synchronized target engagement, employing A-6s, FA-18s, and AC-130s, not over the horizon, but in sight so that everybody could see them. It was just a big firepower demonstration.[27]

Ernst ended his description of the operation with the wonderfully soldierly comment, 'Okay Mohammed [Aidid], we got your message, here's ours.'[28] Aidid was certainly deeply impressed, and although it has never been established that it was this brash display that persuaded him to attend talks in Addis Ababa on national reconciliation, Oakley was able to make available the aircraft that Montgomery had made available to him, and present the spectacle to incredulous observers of Aidid arriving and departing from Mogadishu airport under the angry glare of troops ready at the slightest provocation to shoot him down.

A third operation, the opening of the main 21 October Road that ran through the centre of Mogadishu, which, although superseded somewhat by the bypass road, remained the key line Of communication (LOC) implied in General Ernst's understanding of his mission. The plan was vetoed by Montgomery and was not executed, which ultimately did not interfere with the main objective of the JTF, which was the orderly redeployment of US Forces.

The planned withdrawal had been formally on the table since 24 October when Montgomery had formally assigned Ernst the task. Planning was ongoing, but began to accelerate toward the beginning of December 1993. At this stage, the internal debate within the United Nations regarding the fate of its own mission, once the US and other key coalition partners had withdrawn, reached a fever pitch. This also promoted the last major disagreement between JTF Somalia and USFORSOM. Montgomery wished to retained a viable and robust US force in Somalia through the last stages of redeployment, which Ernst broadly agreed with, but objected to the concentration of force into a redeployment support area adjacent to the airport, citing the obvious troop congestion that would follow, as simply inviting enemy attack. He advocated the removal of more troops and the heavier units earlier than Montgomery would have preferred. Ernst was overruled on the matter and, in December, the Malaysian battalion assumed QRF role and the withdrawal of US forces began along the lines defined by Montgomery and USFORSOM.

On 17 January, Major-General Ernst was redeployed to the United States, at which point Major-General Montgomery removed his blue beret and assumed command of JTF Somalia, which, for the purpose of the withdrawal, was rolled into USFORSOM. There was a certain justice in Major-General Montgomery being the last man out to draw the curtain on a US military operation that had been the first of its kind, and a bitter, but nonetheless valuable lesson in the military/political partnership that would characterize peace missions into the future. He had been involved for over a year, and was arguably the US member with the deepest professional and personal investment in the undertaking. The great moral difficulty of the three missions – UNOSOM, UNITAF and UNOSOM II – had been the fact that the United States military establishment suffered a blow to its reputation that was wholly unjustified. The deportment of the men of Task Force Ranger during the battle of 3 October exemplified all the greatest characteristics of a military culture with a long and proud pedigree. The men of Task Force Ranger did not run from the fight, or shirk from the consequences, or even refuse to re-engage. They were let down by the vacillating political/military leadership and the overarching political agenda that tends to define military campaigning in the modern era.

The phased redeployment continued throughout February and into March. A Marine ground-combat unit came ashore on 4 March to usher out the remaining army task force. By 25 March, all US forces, including JTF headquarters and amphibious forces, had departed from Somalia.

CHAPTER EIGHT: AN AFRICAN SOLUTION FOR AFRICAN PROBLEMS

The world may have bitten off more than it can chew in terms of trying to bring the Somalis to a government
– Daniel Simpson,
US special envoy to Somalia

The US military withdrawal from Somalia removed the main support pillar of the overall UN effort, which quickly began to crumble thereafter. Preceding this, the United States embarked on a diplomatic surge to persuade other nations not to follow suit, but in the realization that this would likely not happen, and set about bolstering a political solution to prepare the way for what would inevitably be a return to a security vacuum. Here again, Robert Oakley assumed the leading role.

It was the US that applied the most direct pressure on the UN to investigate the events of 5 June, and, of course, the arrest order on Aidid was provisionally suspended almost immediately. The force surge that took place in the aftermath of the failed operation of 3 October was intended as a show of force to deter any potential follow-up by Aidid's militias, after which the process of disengagement went ahead as an object lesson in the sheer organizational skill of the US military machine. This was certainly enormously impressive, displaying, once again, the massive power of the US military, but ultimately doing nothing to diffuse the fact that, in real terms, the military game was over. Oakley's principal role now was to set the stage for the nation-building that the United Nations, and everybody else, pinned their hopes upon. It could be reflected upon by those who had been involved in the muscular efforts of the nine months past that conditions in Somalia had improved dramatically under the protection of the international coalition. Agricultural activity had returned to almost normal levels and the widespread starvation that had prompted the effort eradicated; but the fact that the nation, if such it could be called, remained on a knife's edge of inter-factional and clan conflict, shed a very gloomy light on the future, and no matter how optimistic the political prognostications, the aura of overall failure remained acute.

There were multiple and complex policy lessons to be learned by all players in the multi-national humanitarian effort that had been focused on Somalia, most of which have since been absorbed and analyzed in countless UN and inter-agency policy documents, dissertations, books and projections. But perhaps the most visceral conclusion of all was that Africa had a character all of its own in the matter of internal conflict, and if such a vast multi-national effort, which came at an almost incalculable material and human cost, could not impact this comparatively minute family squabble, such as had erupted in Somalia, then clearly there was a cultural

Jan Eliasson

Ethiopian prime minister, Meles Zenawi

Secretary Rice meets with Lansana Kouyate, prime minister of Guinea.

Michael Durant

disconnect of some sort that needed to be taken into account next time a crisis of this nature erupted in Africa. This was borne out less than a month after the last US troops had withdrawn from Somalia, when the comparatively insignificant nation of Rwanda exploded into an orgy of factional violence. Once again, this episode revealed to a bewildered world an incomprehensible ethnic incompatibility in Africa, with its roots obscured by deep history and its contemporary manifestation exacerbated by colonial-era borders that had effectively locked two sworn enemies into one country. The Clinton administration shied away from any direct involvement in this ghastly episode, as did every other major UN donor nation, with the result that three months of orgiastic violence played out across the region, claiming the lives of almost a million people.

There was a forlorn sense of empty process surrounding the organization of the Conference on National Reconciliation in Somalia that took place in Addis Ababa, and which consumed Oakley during the closing weeks and months of 1993. The idea of African solutions to African problems began to emerge as a policy idea at about this time, partly as an admission that non-African efforts had failed, and partly because of some irritation felt at the manifest unwillingness on the part of African governments to dip their toes into the treacherous political waters that the West had so freely plunged into a year earlier, based perhaps on the sense among western donors that the African knew something that they did not.

The popular concept of African Solutions for African Problems emerged as a practical policy direction at about the same time as South Africa prepared to take her place at the table of free nations. Nelson Mandela's release from prison prompted a sense of optimism regarding Africa that briefly replaced the otherwise general and pervasive sense of pessimism. Mandela emerged as a liberation icon, but quickly moved to embrace the role of a functioning statesman charged with the difficult task of bringing to a peaceful end the dying but nonetheless divisive and emotional institution of South African apartheid. The ideal of African governments and leaders rising to the challenges of their own continent, and adopting a philosophy of self-help against a backdrop of international failure, was not at that point quite as forlorn as it had been, and as it would soon be again. The truth of the matter, however, was more prosaic, and had much to do with western governments washing their hands as much as was diplomatically possible of African internal crisis, throwing money at the problems instead of troops, money which African governments were at all times willing to catch and deploy, ostensibly to fuel their own local security resources to fill in the gaps, but, in reality, simply perpetuating a general malaise in the midst of a renewed torrent of international funding.

The pan-African organization of the immediate post-colonial period was the Organization of African Unity, which was inaugurated in Addis Ababa in 1963, but which contained a clause in its charter committing members to the defence of the sovereignty, territorial integrity and independence of member states, which, of course, could easily be translated into a commitment to non-intervention. Bearing in mind the generally tainted legacy of the OAU, this could be further translated into a commitment on the part of a clique of plutocrats to avoid any mutual criticism or interference. It need only be noted that between 1975 and 1976 Ugandan leader, Idi Amin, one of the most high-profile of the lunatic fringe of African post-colonial leadership, served as chairman of the OAU, shattering any credibility that the organization possessed, and certainly defining it as a crony club of fat-cat African politicians/warlords very much in the pattern of Mohammed Farah Aidid himself.

Nonetheless, this is what was hoped, and even if that hope was not substantial, it offered an alternative to the utter hopelessness of what had gone before. The Conference on National Reconciliation in Somalia was organized for 29 November 1993, and was chaired by Jan Eliasson, and guided morally by Somalia's northern neighbour Ethiopia in the person of President Meles Zenawi.* His message was simple and to the point. A continuation of the current levels of violence in Somalia would result in the abandonment of the country by the world community, and an inheritance of state when it was finally resolved that would represent nothing so much

* Jan Eliason at that time was serving as 1st under-secretary-general for Humanitarian Affairs and emergency relief coordinator

Saudi Arabian vehicles waiting for food stores to be offloaded at the Mogadishu port. The food will be provided to the Somali people.

as a shell of a country. Similarly, donor representatives stated their willingness to commit the necessary resources to rebuild the country, but that, again, fundamental security guarantees would be required if the nation was not to be abandoned.

This initially prompted a certain amount of determined bargaining among the Somali factions, with no major clashes taking place in Mogadishu, or elsewhere, while focus remained on politics. At the same time, the UN secretary-general made a recommendation to the Security Council to scale back UNOSOM's mission, emphasizing the need to encourage cooperation between the factions and reinforcing the objectives of the humanitarian conference, all of which appeared to shine some small ray of hope that all might not be lost. It was made clear that the focus would now be on Somali initiatives and, although coercive disarmament remained Boutros-Ghali's preferred option, he finally recognized that this was practically impossible in the light of a general haemorrhage of substantive international troop contingents in Somalia. Voluntary disarmament, for all the improbability of that, became his second choice, and thus the expectation was accepted that Somalia would, into the foreseeable future, remain armed and dangerous. United Nations security responsibilities would return to a simple oversight of port, convoy and refugee protection, with the proviso that this would be dealt with, and would be dependent upon, cooperation with the Somali parties.

In the meanwhile, efforts to keep some foreign troops on the ground required much diplomatic trench work on the part of the Clinton administration. Notwithstanding the strong smell of irony that this stirred up, the deal was sweetened by the provision of equipment, such as armoured personnel carriers and smaller ordnance that nations would likely take home with them. The most substantial forces to remain in the country were the Italians and the Pakistanis but, besides these, only such nations as India, Egypt, Zimbabwe, Morocco, Botswana and Malaysia opted to remain, and Montgomery and Bir were replaced by Malaysian general, Aboo Samah Bin-Aboo Baker, and Zimbabwean general, Michael Nayambua respectively. Retired Admiral Howe was recalled and ultimately replaced by Guinean diplomat, Lansana Kouyaté.

Aidid, meanwhile, began to make presidential noises, being careful at the same time not to interfere with the free flow of foreign troops out of Somalia. Twenty thousand international troops remained in the country, however, under a much-reduced mandate, and with the broad if superficial endorsement of the Somali factions. Ambassador Kouyaté worked tirelessly to limit the local powerplay among the warlords and clan leaders that went on beneath the surface of considerably less robust internationally brokered understandings. Levels of violence began to escalate as UNSOM II continued to close in on itself, in tight, protective formations, with very little interest being shown in projecting force. UN casualties mounted, notably among Indian forces in and around Kismayo, but also including five Nepalese soldiers

A US Air Force C-130 Hercules delivering pallets of humanitarian aid.

killed when caught in the crossfire between two feuding factions in Mogadishu. By mid-1994, UN convoys were, once again, frequently being ambushed while the number of 'technicals' and general armaments evident on the streets of the capital crept, more or less, back to pre-UNITAF levels.

The UN, meanwhile, although responding to the inevitable with the usual exchanges of verbiage and public handwringing, arrived eventually at the unavoidable conclusion that the situation in Somalia was hopeless. The UNOSOM mandate was extended to 30 September, while, at the same time, force levels were further reduced and UNOSOM's activities narrowed even further. The US Department of State announced the closure of the US liaison office and the removal of all official US personnel from Somalia by mid-September. This, probably more than anything, sounded the death knell for UNOSOM, and any substantive hope for an ordered solution to the Somalia crisis evaporated. As international units were rotated out of the country, many were not replaced, while the practicalities of an ordered withdrawal began increasingly to dominate discussion at the United Nations.

This prompted an interest among Somalis in general, and the warlords in particular, in seizing as much in the way of UN civil and military assets as possible. Mobs began to assemble at the gates of the sea port in the Bermuda district of Mogadishu, where persistent and characteristically fearless efforts were made to gain access to the perimeter in order to seize what could be seized, in particular military hardware, much of it of US origin, but also UN and aid organization vehicles, food and general equipment. As UN troops stationed around the capital, Pakistanis mainly, began abandoning their positions and making their way to the airport, where all the multi-national contingents were scheduled to muster, the Somalis closed in almost immediately behind them and began the process of stripping down and looting every movable, and many immovable assets, such as building supplies and fixtures from the various UN complexes. According to George Bennett, the United Nations spokesman on the ground: 'As soon as they [United Nations personnel] moved out, the Somalis moved in and started taking all the equipment that was left.'[29]

Eye-witness and news reports of the period paint an extremely bleak picture of Aidid's 'technicals' and militiamen taking up positions surrounding the UN complex as staff were escorted out, with armed men and civilians very quickly moving in room by room, carrying away in any available transport, food, bottled water, window frames, roofing sheets, electrical and plumbing fixtures and anything else that could be torn up and carted off. As the UN trucks rolled out of sight, squabbles began to break out, with sporadic gunfire punctuating the frenzy in a scene of almost primordial simplicity, reminiscent perhaps of vultures bickering over the corpse of a newly dead enterprise. A battle was initiated as Bangladeshi troops attempted to leave their base north of Mogadishu to relocate to the airport. The departing convoy was attacked because clan leaders negotiating rent for land felt that the cash settlement was insufficient. Later in the same week, a number of United Nations workers were held hostage for several hours by armed Somali security guards dissatisfied with their severance packages. The whole episode must have been extremely depressing for those that had invested such blood, hope and treasure in an attempt to elevate the people of this country from such an elemental standard of existence as now appeared to once again overwhelm them.

The official date for the final withdrawal of UNOSOM II from Somalia was set at 31 March 1995. At the urging of the joint chiefs of staff, it was decided that US forces would return briefly to the theatre in order to assist with the withdrawal, in part as an acknowledgement that the US had been instrumental in persuading those incumbent forces to remain, but also to ensure that US and allied military equipment did not fall into the hands of the warring factions. CENTCOM and the Pacific Marine Forces were once again assigned to the task, and, on 8 February, CENTCOM assumed command of all forces identified to participate in the withdrawal. Italy and France also volunteered troops to assist. In late January, an advance party of 160 Marines arrived in Mogadishu to help UN forces expedite the withdrawal, with a further 7,000 to 8,000 naval and military personnel earmarked to take part, but remaining offshore for the time being. Of these, 3,000 Marines were assigned to cover the pull-out. These were commanded by General Zinni and assisted by a small contingent of Italian marines. They would not make landfall on Somali soil until the first week of March, by which time the 4,500 remaining UN troops would be concentrated at the port and the airport ready for departure.

In the meanwhile, sporadic actions between the two factions erupted into severe fighting as both sides jostled for advantage in gaining ultimate control of the key strategic points of the capital in the aftermath of the pending withdrawal – the airport and the port area primarily – with both zones tending to pass back and forth between the factions, as the balance of power swung, and as international forces hurried to depart as quickly and cleanly as the very dirty situation would allow. Without making public the actual timetable for withdrawal, UN troops continued to be quietly withdrawn for outlying bases and mustered at key staging areas in Mogadishu, Kismayo and Baidoa. The first contingent scheduled for embarkation as transport became available was the 4,700-man Indian force concentrated in Kismayo, by then almost under siege as fighting began to overwhelm the city as the factions fought to decide who would fill the vacuum. By 11 December, the city had been effectively abandoned as the last of the Indian battalions boarded commercial vessels and left the city under the protection of the Indian navy, transiting thereafter to Mogadishu where about 15,000 troops were gathered in preparation for the final departure. In the midst of it all, news reached Somalia of the death of Siad Barre, who had succumbed to a heart attack in Lagos, Nigeria on 2 January 1995. His body was returned to Somalia and buried in the Garbahaarreey district of the Gedo region in Somalia, in the midst of the UN withdrawal.

During the pre-dawn hours of Tuesday, 28 February, 1,800 US and Italian marines landed on the shores of Mogadishu to provide the rearguard for the final withdrawal of the last of the United Nations peacekeepers, again, mainly Pakistanis. The 72-hour operation ended without casualties, although several fusillades of warning fire were directed at Somali 'technical' crews probing the perimeters of the narrow US zone. More than one Somali militiaman was taken out by Marine sniper fire as hostile advances continued. Once the last of the Pakistanis had left Somali soil, 15 US amphibious vehicles carried the marine rearguard into the surf and towards the naval flotilla that awaited them, covered overhead by helicopter crews and an AC-130 Specter gunship. And thus, with a profound lack of ceremony, the saga ended.

In the meanwhile, notwithstanding the fact that Somali police assumed brief control of both the port and the airport, it soon became clear that both major Somali factions were positioning themselves for a renewed contest over supremacy of the capital.* Military observers, pondering an increase in the price of ammunition and armaments on the Somali black market, speculated that fighting would need to be restrained, but that a renewal of violence on some level was inevitable as the last foreign troops left the theatre.

In fact, as February had progressed, and as the deadline of the withdrawal approached, the sporadic clashes that had been ongoing for some time quickly solidified into a significant action, fought almost at the gates of the airport, spraying the complex with gunfire even as foreign troops were being moved out into waiting air and sea transports. A mortar shell landed within 200 yards of a Boeing 747 that was loading Pakistani troops, with another landing in the complex of the United Nations special envoy, Victor Gbeho, killing one Somali policeman. The US helicopter landing zone was moved beyond the airport, behind the dunes adjacent to the beach, while Pakistani armoured troop carriers, previously lined up at the port for loading onto ships, were returned to the airport and the perimeter of the port, where they were placed in defensive positions as the withdrawal continued.

Supporting the Pakistani and Bangladeshi troops as they attempted to secure the perimeter of the seaport and the airport were 50 members of the Fifth Special Forces Group based out of Fort Campbell, Kentucky. According to a report in the *New York Times*:

> They [the special force members] have observed the daily changes as the Somali militias have positioned themselves outside the gates in a constant cat-and-mouse game. Today they were close enough to see the muzzle flashes from the Soviet anti-aircraft gun and the 50-calibre machine gun mounted on the back of a pick-up truck that opened fire on another nearby armed truck of the kind known here as 'technicals'.[30]

* A brief effort to return a civilian police force to the streets of the capital formed part of the attempt at nation-building. It did not survive.

The career of Mohamed Farah Aidid continued, with his unilateral declaration a few months after the UN withdrawal of his own presidency of Somalia, which obviously did not achieve international recognition. On 24 July 1996, however, he was injured in a gunfight between his militia and those of Ali Mahdi and Osman Ali Atto, a former ally who had since turned against him. Aidid was wounded and suffered a heart attack, either during or after surgery, which ultimately caused his death. His heir, in a final twist of irony, was his son, Hussein Mohamed Farah Aidid, a naturalized citizen of the United States and an ex-member of the Marine Corps. Hussein Mohamed Farah Aidid had been an obvious choice to serve as part of UNITAF for his bilingualism. He returned to Somalia in 1996 and was selected by the Habar Gidir as his father's successor and, although transmogrifying quickly into a warlord of the standard Somali pattern, he was seen as a possible vehicle to introduce a more rational political process. It is arguable whether anything of this sort was achieved.

UN APCs around the UNOSOM university compound in Mogadishu.

Above and middle: the UNOSOM compound in Mogadishu.

In the period since, peace and stable governance has eluded Somalia and, in many respects, the country has limped from crisis to crisis, emerging as the quintessential African failed state, and existing without any recognizable government since the ouster of Siad Barre. In the age of Islamofascism, Somalia, in many respects, has been on the front line, with Islamic fundamentalism seeping into the Somali narrative in the form of the Al-Shabaab movement, which was recognized in 2012 as a cell of the global militant Islamist organisation al Qaeda. Somalia has also been the base and centre of operations of Indian Ocean piracy, further reinforcing the emerging popular image of the country as essentially a pirate state. So far, all efforts to introduce stability and rule of law into the country have failed, with the latest entrant into the débâcle being Kenya, which has, in recent months, entered Somali in an effort to buffer its own border with the rogue state, as increasing predations have tended to suck it into the vortex of insecurity in the region.

In contrast, the northern self-declared Republic of Somaliland remains relatively stable and well administered, and has, so far, succeeded in remaining aloof from the ongoing crisis that has engulfed its southern neighbour. Somalia does host a central government of sorts, that has been sustained against the odds, albeit with almost no real authority, but this seed of organization in the midst of chaos has spread tenuous roots, and grown into a slender sapling. However, against the whirlwind of violence and internal strife, the effort remains an extremely fragile hope indeed.

APPENDIX I: UH-60 BLACK HAWK SPECIFICATIONS

The UH-60 Black Hawk is a utility tactical transport helicopter introduced to replace the Bell UH-1 *Huey*. It features dramatic improvements in troop capacity and cargo-lift capability, and is expected to serve as The US Army's main utility helicopter until 2025/30.

Manufacturer	Sikorsky Aircraft
Performance	Max Cruise Speed
	4,000ft; 95°F 152 knots
	2,000ft; 70°F 159 knots
	SLS 155 knots
	VNE 193 knots
Vertical Rate of Climb	95% MRP
	4,000ft; 95°F 1,550ft per minute
	2,000ft; 70°F 2,750ft per minute
	SLS > 3,000ft per minute
Service Ceiling	(ISA day) 19,1510ft
	Hover Ceiling MRP-OGE
	95°F 7,650ft
	70°F 9,375ft
	Standard Day 11,125ft
Weight	Empty 11,516lbs
	Mission gross weight: 17,432lbs
	Maximum gross weight: 22,000lbs
	Maximum gross weight (ferry): 24,500lbs
Length	64ft 10in
Height	16ft 10in
Rotor	Diameter: 53ft 8in
	Four titanium and fiberglass blades

APPENDIX II: CHRONOLOGY 3/4 OCTOBER 1993

13h00 - ISA agent reports that several key SNA lieutenants are planning a meeting at 15h00
15h30 - TFR boards helicopters
15h40 - TFR initiates the raid
15h45 - Rangers establish security
16h00 - Delta commandos secure prisoners
16h10 - Super 61 shot down by SNA RPGs
16h15 - Lt-Col McKnight ordered to bring prisoners back to airfield
16h20 - Super 64 shot down by SNA RPGs
16h30 - Lt-Col David ordered back to the airfield
17h24 - Lt-Col David arrives at airfield
17h47 - Lt-Col David leads first rescue mission
17h54 - Rescue force comes under heavy fire
18h21 - Lt-Col David ordered back to airfield
18h30 - Super 61 attempts rescue of Super 64 crew
19h10 - Lt-Col David arrives back at airfield
22h45 - Pakistani and Malaysian armored forces arrive at airfield for mission briefing
23h24 - Second rescue mission initiated
00h24 - Relief column splits up
01h55 - First column arrives at TFR perimeter
02h00 - Second column arrives at Super 64
05h30 - Rescue convoy reaches Pakistani base

The crew of a Black Hawk helicopter perform their pre-flight checks.

APPENDIX III: US RANGERS

The term 'ranger' in the historical sense implies a backwoodsman proficient in stealth and survival, and used in the military context in tracking, guerrilla action and what might be termed 'special operations'. This certainly defines a large section of the early American frontier population, and the style of warfare employed against the British during the Revolutionary War (The Corps of Ranger), and in various Indian Wars, as the frontier was pushed forward, made use of many men regarded as Rangers.

The 1st Ranger Battalion was formed as a limited unit of elite volunteer infantrymen on 8 June 1942, under the command of Major William Orlando Darby, operating initially under the informal name of Darby's Rangers. The first major operation involving the Ranger Battalion was the ill-fated raid on Dieppe that took place on 19 August 1942.

Full regimental status was awarded to the unit soon afterward, with the creation of additional battalions, the 3rd and 4th battalions, which were trained by men drawn from the 1st. The almost complete annihilation of the battalions took place during a side battle of Operation Shingle, fought as part of the Anzio campaign in January 1944. The battle of Cisterna claimed the lives of all but six of the 750 members of the 1st and 3rd battalions. The 400 surviving members of the regiment were assimilated into the elite 504th Parachute Regiment, with the 137 original members returning home. On 26 October 1944, the three original Ranger battalions were deactivated at the now defunct Camp Butner in North Carolina.

The 2nd and 5th Ranger battalions were trained at Camp Forrest, Tennessee during April 1943 and arrived in theatre in time to see action during Operation Overlord. The 6th Ranger Battalion was stationed in the Pacific, serving primarily in company or platoon formation behind enemy lines in the Philippines and New Guinea.

The unit further evolved during the Korean and Vietnam wars, with 17 Korean War Ranger companies being formed during the former from the Ranger Training Programme established at Fort Benning, Georgia, under Colonel John Gibson Van Houten. The companies that were formed during this period were the first to be entirely airborne qualified.

At the end of the Vietnam War, division and brigade commanders recognized that the US Army needed an elite, rapid-deployment light infantry. The 1st Ranger Battalion was created in 1974, by General Creighton Abrams, and was assigned its lineage from C Company (Ranger) 75th Infantry (Airborne) First Field Force Vietnam. The 2nd Ranger Battalion was formed eight months later with the lineage of H Company (Ranger) 75th Infantry (Airborne), 1st Cavalry Division, Vietnam. It was not until a decade later, 1984, that the 3rd Ranger Battalion, and the regimental headquarters, were created. Two years later, in 1986, the 75th Ranger Regiment was established and its lineage formally authorized. The 4th, 5th, and 6th Ranger battalions were also re-activated, becoming the Ranger Training Brigade, the progenitor of the modern-day Ranger School. These units form part of United States Army Training and Doctrine Command (TRADOC) school, and are excluded from the 75th Ranger Regiment.

Consequent to the evolving nature of modern warfare and the need for an agile and sustainable Ranger Force, the Regimental Special Troops Battalion (RSTB) was activated on 17 July 2006. The RSTB conducts sustainment, intelligence, reconnaissance and maintenance missions, which were previously accomplished by small detachments assigned to the regimental headquarters and then attached within each of the three Ranger battalions.

Rangers parachute from a US Air Force C-17 Globemaster III.

APPENDIX IV: RANGER CREED

Recognizing that I volunteered as a Ranger, fully knowing the hazards of my chosen profession, I will always endeavor to uphold the prestige, honour, and high esprit de corps of my Ranger Regiment.

Acknowledging the fact that a Ranger is a more elite soldier who arrives at the cutting edge of battle by land, sea, or air, I accept the fact that as a Ranger my country expects me to move further, faster and fight harder than any other soldier.

Never shall I fail my comrades. I will always keep myself mentally alert, physically strong, and morally straight and I will shoulder more than my share of the task, whatever it may be, one hundred per cent and then some.

Gallantly will I show the world that I am a specially selected and well-trained soldier. My courtesy to superior officers, neatness of dress, and care of equipment shall set the example for others to follow.

Energetically will I meet the enemies of my country. I shall defeat them on the field of battle for I am better trained and will fight with all my might. Surrender is not a Ranger word. I will never leave a fallen comrade to fall into the hands of the enemy and under no circumstances will I ever embarrass my country.

Readily will I display the intestinal fortitude required to fight on to the Ranger objective and complete the mission, though I be the lone survivor.

A US Army soldier assigned to the 1st Battalion, 75th Ranger Regiment, provides supporting fire while participating in a combined-arms live-fire exercise near Fort Stewart, Georgia.

NOTES

[1] Burton, Richard Francis. *First Footsteps in East Africa* (Longman, Brown, Green & Longmans, London. 1856) p. 123

[2] Stevenson, Jonathan. *Losing Mogadishu* (Naval Institute Press, Annapolis, Maryland, 1995) p. 1

[3] Hirsch, John L. & Oakley, Robert B. *Somalia and Operation Restore Hope: Reflections on Peacemaking and Peacekeeping.*(United States Institute of Peace Press, Washington DC, 1995) p. 6

[4] USCinCCent mss, dd 22 November 1992: 'Commander's Estimate of the Situation'

[5] Mroczkowski, Colonel Dennis P. *Restoring Hope: In Somalia with the Unified Task Force, 1992–1993* (History Division, United States Marine Corps, Washington, D.C. 2005) pp. 22-3

[6] Stevenson. p. 11

[7] Allard, Kenneth. *Somalia Operations: Lessons Learned.* (CCRP Publications) p. 66

[8] *Ibid.* p. 63

[9] Schilling, Dan. *The Battle of Mogadishu: Firsthand Accounts From the Men of Task Force Ranger.*(Presido Press. New York, 2006) p. 184

[10] Gordon, Michael R. 'US Officers were divided on Somali Raid'. *New York Times*, 13 May 1994

[11] *Ibid*

[12] Sangvic, Major Roger N. Monograph: 'Battle of Mogadishu: Anatomy of Failure'

[13] *Ibid*

[14] Bowden, Mark. *Black Hawk Down* (Bantam Press, London, 2000) pp. 118-9

[15] Baumann, Robert F., Yates, Lawrence A. & Washington, Versalle F. Gen Montgomery, quoted: *My Clan Against the World: US Coalition Forces in Somalia, 1992–1994* (Combat Studies Institute Press. Ft. Leavenworth, Kansas) p. 169

[16] Hirsch & Oakley. p. 131

[17] Bowden. p. 476

[18] Casper, Lawrence E. *Falcon Brigade: Combat and Command in Somalia and Haiti* (Lynne Rienner Publishers. Boulder/London 2001) p. 102

[19] *Ibid.* p. 11

[20] *Ibid.* p. 24

[21] *Ibid.* p. 102

[22] *Ibid.* p. 103

[23] Baumann, Robert F., Yates, Lawrence A. & Washington, Versalle F. Gen Montgomery, quoted. p. 192

[24] Allard. p. 75

[25] Baumann, Robert F., Yates, Lawrence A. & Washington, Versalle F. Gen Montgomery, quoted. p. 192

[26] Casper. p. 111

[27] Ernst, MG Carl F., U.S. Army (ret.), 'The Urban Area During Support Missions Case Study: Mogadishu: The Operational Level'

[28] *Ibid*

[29] *New York Times*, 2 February 1995

[30] *Ibid*, 26 February 1995

Peter Baxter is an author, amateur historian and African field, mountain and heritage travel guide. Born in Kenya and educated in Zimbabwe, he has lived and travelled over much of southern and central Africa. He has guided in all the major mountain ranges south of the equator, helping develop the concept of sustainable travel, and the touring of battlefield and heritage sites in East Africa. Peter lives in Oregon, USA, working on the marketing of African heritage travel as well as a variety of book projects. His interests include British Imperial history in Africa and the East Africa campaign of the First World War in particular. His first book was *Rhodesia: Last Outpost of the British Empire*; he has written several books in the Africa@War series, including *France in Centrafrique*, *Selous Scouts*, *Mau Mau* and *SAAF's Border War.*